What's Good About Anger?
Expanded Book & Workbook for Teens
How to Cope with Anger, Conflict, Aggression, Hostility & Bullying
(Second Edition)

©copyright 2016 by Lynette J. Hoy, NCC, LCPC, CAMS-V
&
Ted Griffin, Editor/writer

A CounselCare Connection Publication
Oak Brook, Illinois
www.counselcareconnection.org

May be purchased at the
Anger Management Institute shopping mall:
www.whatsgoodaboutanger.com

What's Good About Anger?
Expanded Book & Workbook for Teens
How to Cope with Anger, Conflict, Aggression, Hostility & Bullying
(Second Edition)

Copyright © 2016 by Lynette J. Hoy and Ted Griffin;
Adapted from original, second, third, fourth edition
What's Good About Anger? books

Requests for information should be addressed to:
CounselCare Connection P.C.
1200 Harger Road, Suite 602
Oak Brook, Illinois 60523
Original printing, 2002
Second edition, 2006
Third edition, 2012
Fourth edition, 2016

ISBN: 978-1530806362

Unless otherwise indicated, Scripture quotations are from the ESV® Bible (The Holy Bible, English Standard Version®), copyright © 2001 by Crossway Bibles, a publishing ministry of Good News Publishers. Used by permission. All rights reserved.

All rights reserved. No part of this book may be reproduced or transmitted in any form or by any means, electronic or mechanical, including photocopying, recording, or any information storage and retrieval system—except for brief quotations in printed reviews, without the prior permission of the publisher/authors.

CounselCare Connection Publications
Oak Brook, Illinois
Printed in the United States of America

To my lovely wife Lois, for her gracious patience and persevering love, without which I might never have chosen to allow God to bring my anger under his control.
　　Ted Griffin

To my husband, David, who has inspired and encouraged me and demonstrated God's love to me for over 46 years.
　　Lynette J. Hoy

What's Good About Anger? Expanded Book & Workbook for Teens

TABLE OF CONTENTS

Introduction and overview	5
Anger Survey	8
1: Anger's many faces	13
2: The power of anger	21
3: What is good about anger?	31
4: Defusing anger by managing stress	37
5: Handling anger effectively	47
6: Anger and assertiveness	53
7: Managing conflict	61
8: Turn your anger into forgiveness	69
9: When to take a 'Break'	77
10: Plan to change your life by changing your thinking	81
11: How emotional intelligence impacts anger	91
12: Building healthy and successful relationships	101
13: Choosing behavior alternatives	105
14: Defusing anger & hostility. Dealing with Bullying	109
15: Accepting responsibility for unhealthy anger	123
16: Facing the consequences of and interrupting aggression	127
Anger Management Progress Report	132
Case Study: Bob	133
Appendix: Assertiveness Scenarios, Cognitive Strategies & Belief Inventory	137
Notes	144
Bibliography	145
About the Authors & Resources	146

What's Good About Anger? Expanded Book & Workbook for Teens (Second Edition)

Introduction: Everyone who reads this book is looking for answers to anger. Whether it is for yourself or someone else – anger has impacted your life negatively. This new second edition book for teens is based on the 2016 edition of What's Good About Anger? and includes questions and activities geared to *help you find healthy solutions to destructive anger*.

It is our goal that you will grow in understanding more about anger, how to manage it effectively and how to express your anger in healthy ways. Healthy anger can help you achieve your goals and build your relationships.

Read through and complete the questions and assignments found in this book. Start out by completing the survey, logging your scenarios and anger, thinking patterns and answering the thought questions at the end of the lessons. This will help you discover what makes you angry, what coping skills you use to manage it and what new approaches you may need to apply to your own life.

Reflect on this question: *What makes people angry?*
Numerous answers may come to mind such as:

> Differences of opinion
> Personality clashes
> Expectations
> Blocked goals
> Low self-esteem
> Depression, grief, mental health disorders
> Loss of hope and control
> Health problems
> Conflict
> School or work dissatisfaction
> Financial pressures
> Stress
> Family or relationship issues

Anger is a common emotion for everyone and thus, you will find as you read that many people experience anger: people who are depressed or withdrawn; those who tend to hold in their feelings, hurt and anger or lash out and are aggressive when they feel angry. Often it is taught that anger is not an acceptable emotion or experience for religious people, but, through this course you will come to understand *What's Good About Anger.*

Overview:

The What's Good About Anger? course will give you a fresh look at anger and explore how this emotion--usually viewed as destructive--can be helpful and be transformed into assertiveness, problem-solving, empathy, conflict resolution and forgiveness.

Chronic anger can be costly-- physically, emotionally and relationally. Most people can use their anger in appropriate ways in some situations, and yet can be ineffectual or harmful in other situations. Participation in this course can reduce levels of anger, and help individuals learn to turn their anger into productive behaviors, faith and forgiveness. You can learn effective coping behaviors to stop escalation and to resolve conflicts. Logging anger, triggering situations and applying new coping approaches will help you to more effectively control unhealthy anger responses.

This anger management course employs these major areas and anger control interventions:

- Identifying triggers,
- Logging scenarios,
- Applying new skills such as: time-outs, prayer,
- Addressing issues with assertiveness,
- Establishing a plan of action,
- Making requests,
- Learning to problem-solve,
- Getting guidance from a pastor or counselor when needed,
- Changing self-talk,
- Conflict resolution,
- Stress management,
- Relaxation techniques,
- Emotional Intelligence & empathy skills,
- Turning anger into forgiveness,
- Managing stress and conflict,
- Changing behavior,
- Dealing with control issues,
- Taking responsibility,
- Stopping aggression.

Here are the instructions as you use the What's Good About Anger? Course with additional guidelines:

1. Complete the Anger Survey. This will help you assess when, where and *how* you get angry and your general provocation scenario (GPS). Be honest about your feelings and experience with anger. After all, this course-work is personal and geared to help you get an understanding of how you can grow in tackling any problem you may be having with anger in your life and in your relationships.

2. Complete the Anger Management Progress Report found in this course each week to keep track of any improvements you are making.

3. Then read through this course, completing the questions and any activities as you progress. Apply your general provocation scenario (found in the Anger Survey) to the lesson on Handling Anger Effectively.

4. Keep an anger log throughout the time you are reading this course. Each day think about and try one or two of the suggestions for handling anger. Especially apply the steps in "Handling Anger Effectively" to each situation. Write out your basic concerns, your options and requests.

5. Carefully, read through the lessons on assertiveness, stress management, conflict management and forgiveness. Apply these concepts and skills to your personal life and relationships.

6. Read "When to Take a Break" in order to plan for the situations that tend to cause anger to escalate and feelings that you are losing control. If you still find your anger escalating, then lengthen your time-out period (Example: one hour instead of 30 minutes).

7. Evaluate your thinking with the cognitive distortions questions and log your thinking patterns. This exercise will help you identify any false perspective and thinking you may have about people or situations and motivate you to change those patterns. Complete the Plan to Change Your Life By Changing Your Thinking.

8. Read the lesson on How Emotional Intelligence (EI) Impacts Anger. This lesson will help you learn how to develop EI as you apply the various anger management strategies to your life and relationships!

9. Most importantly, complete the thought questions for each lesson. What If? questions, activity sheets and assertive scenarios can be found through-out this book & workbook to help you think through and apply the skills which are most effective for managing and transforming your anger.

All aspects of this course – defusing anger and hostility, bullying, taking responsibility, dealing with consequences, preventing aggression -- will encourage you to apply helpful strategies and foundational principles to your life so you can *put your anger to work for good!*

Now – let's get started by completing the anger survey on the next page.

What's Good About Anger? Expanded Book & Workbook for Teens

ANGER SURVEY © copyright 2016 by Lynette J. Hoy, NCC, LCPC and Ted Griffin, Editor/writer
Please answer the following questions as accurately and as completely as possible.

Rate the severity of your anger:

1. **How often do you get angry?**
(Circle one that applies)
(a) daily
(b) many times a day
(c) a few times a month
(d) several times a week
(e) very rarely

Question 1:

(a) 4
(b) 5
(c) 2
(d) 3
(e) 1

2. **What happens when you get angry?**
(Circle all that apply)
I tend to:
(a) feel tense
(b) withdraw
(c) exercise
(d) feel sick
(e) overeat
(f) distract myself
(g) tell someone
(h) raise my voice
(i) hit someone or something
(j) become cynical or sarcastic
(k) take a time-out
(l) think about how to get even
(m) avoid the issue
(n) make light of things or joke
(o) pray
(p) other_____
(q) go out drinking
(r) argue
(s) talk it over
(t) swear
(u) feel depressed

Question 2:

(a) 1
(b) 3
(c) 1
(d) 3
(e) 3
(f) 1
(g) 1
(h) 4
(i) 5
(j) 4
(k) 1
(l) 4
(m) 3
(n) 3
(o) 0
(p) 3 (if a negative or harmful response)
(q) 5
(r) 4
(s) 1
(t) 4
(u) 4

Total your scores from questions 1 and 2 together.
Assess the category you are in:

Category I: 1-10 points = little problem with anger.
Category II: 10-20 points = moderate problem.
*If either Category I or II includes trouble with the law, injury to others or self, drinking, depression, outbursts, experiencing anger several times a day, etc. then, you have a serious--Category III problem with anger.
Category III: 20 points and above = serious problem with anger.

Resource: What's Good About Anger? ©copyright 2016 by Lynette J. Hoy, NCC, LCPC and Ted Griffin, Editor/writer.

What's Good About Anger? Expanded Book & Workbook for Teens

3. **Which people tend to trigger your anger?** (check or circle all that apply):
___(a) significant others
___(b) students (or co-workers)
___(c) policemen
___(d) parents
___(e) friends
___(f) strangers
___(g) men
___(h) women
___(i) others: (teachers)_____

4. **What situations or behavior tend to trigger your anger?** (check all that apply):
When people:
___(a) treat me unfairly
___(b) disrespect me
___(c) ignore me
___(d) put me down
___(e) threaten me
___(f) interrupt me
___(g) keep me waiting
___(h) joke about me
___(i) hit me

When I am:
___(j) at school or working
___(k) disappointed with someone
___(l) missing someone
___(m) experiencing loss or change
___(n) under stress
___(o) late to events
___(p) unable to achieve my goals
___(q) unable to share my opinions
___(r) bored
___(s) in a crisis
___(t) Other: _____

Write out a recent situation when you felt angry:
What happened?

Where was it? How long did you feel angry?

With whom were you angry?

How did you react?

5. **Where are you most likely to get angry?** (check all that apply):
___(a) at home
___(b) at school or work
___(c) in social situations
___(d) during sports or recreation activities
___(e) driving
___(f) in public
___(g) other:_____

6. **What happens after you get angry?** (check all that apply):
___(a) someone gets hurt
___(b) I feel guilty
___(c) my relationships are disrupted
___(d) I feel defensive
___(e) I get in trouble with the law
___(f) I try to make restitution or reconcile with the person
___(g) I ask God for wisdom and guidance
___(h) I don't talk to the other person
___(i) I can't stop thinking about the event/person
___(j) I get depressed or think about harming myself
___(k) I lose sleep or can't eat
___(l) I feel relieved
___(m) I have been asked to leave
___(n) I get in trouble at school/work
___(o) others say I have a problem with anger
___(p) I want to run away
___(q) other: _____

Rate your answers from question 6 above.
.....You handle anger *pretty well* if you checked only b, f, g and l.
   Anger is not disrupting your life but, you could be dealing with hidden anger.
.....You are unable to control your anger and your anger is *causing serious interference in* your life and relationships
   if you checked any of these:
   a, c, e, h, i, j, k, m, n, o, p, and (q: if *other* is an unhealthy response).

7. **How do you normally help yourself calm down when you feel angry?** (check all that apply):
___(a) deep breathing and relaxation techniques
___(b) prayer
___(c) counting to ten
___(d) reading inspirational books
___(e) telling myself: This is not worth getting angry over
___(f) thinking about the negative consequences that could result from getting angry and losing control
___(g) thinking about what the real issue is

I tell myself:
___(h) This person is not making sense now. He/she may have had a bad day
___(i) I'm going to try to work through this problem reasonably
___(j) I should try to cooperate – he's/she's making sense
___(k) Maybe I should take a time-out until I cool down
___(l) I should try to understand what this person is upset about by listening and paraphrasing
Other things you say or do to control yourself or the situation:_____

General Provocation Scenario: In the space below write out a typical situation which you find yourself getting annoyed or angry. Pretend it is a play. Describe what happened, who was involved, when and where it happened and what transpired beforehand. Then write out what each person said and did and what you thought, communicated and how you acted.

Who:

Where:

When:

What led up to this scene:

The scene opens:

What I think:

What I do:

What I say:

What other person says/does:

How did you recently control or not control your anger?

Write out: What happened?

What triggered your angry response?

What were the circumstances?

What were your thoughts?

What were you telling yourself?

Who else was involved?

Log Your Anger:

Write down the situations when you get angry, and rate them:

1. When did you last feel angry?

2. What happened and with whom?

3. What were you thinking when this occurred?
Example: "He/she never understands." "I am just a failure." "I can't handle this." "He/she doesn't care about me." "This situation is hopeless." "I will never succeed." "That person meant to ignore me." "This project is dead in the water." "I couldn't have done a worse job."
"That person never should have cut me off." "If I had just prayed more, I never would have gotten suspended." "He's such a loser."

4. Rate the strength of the anger: 1 = lowest; 5 = moderate; 10 = strongest.

       1   2   3   4   5   6   7   8   9   10

5. Continue to keep an anger log for one to two weeks, then, evaluate your angry responses as suggested below.

What could you have changed?

Did you take any time-outs to cool down?

Evaluate your angry response:
How did it affect you and others?
Was it destructive; did it lead to resentment and broken relationships?

Did it lead to problem-solving, restoring relationships, and honest (loving) dialogue?

Did you seek spiritual help or counsel?

What would help you control your anger in the future?

What was your thinking prior to and during the episode of anger? Do you have any of the Cognitive Distortions found in the course?

Now go to "Handling Anger Effectively," and apply your situations to the model given.

Lesson One: Anger's Many Faces

Goal: To define anger, how it affects people and relationships. To explore triggers for and teaching about anger.

Anger, though potentially harmful, can be transformed into a positive force accomplishing great good in our lives.

Ted Griffin and Lynette Hoy

Lynette's Story

I can remember the day one of my sisters came home with a suspension slip for throwing an orange in the lunchroom. My father dragged her upstairs to the attic. There were loud noises, yelling, and crying. She limped down the stairs, bloody and bruised.

I can remember the beatings in the basement with a board, my father's rage, the pain and the fear.

I can remember experiencing a "cold shoulder" for days when I would disappoint someone in my family.

I can remember my husband and I up in the attic of our second story rented flat, two weeks after our daughter was born, screaming at each other and throwing things. I don't remember what caused the anger or why it hurt so much. But I experienced anger's pain, inner wounds, and loneliness.

I learned that anger was something to be feared, that it was cruel, loud, cold, silent, resentful, and threatening.

Ted's Story

I have long feared anger--my father's and my own. My dad, an alcoholic who's drinking kept him from connecting with his family, had a quiet anger. He didn't beat us or yell at us for hours-he just sort of ignored us. My anger--which was really years' worth of bitterness toward Dad--became violent, abusive and dangerous, especially after my father died and I couldn't express my anger to the one I was really mad at because he wasn't around anymore.

Looking back, I am ashamed of many of the things I said and did at that stage of my life. And I thank God for helping me forgive my father and learn how to be kind to my family--a family I almost lost because of my rage. Not all anger is wrong, but when it's like mine was, only God can keep the individual and his family from going over the cliff. The journey hasn't been easy or quick, but God has sustained me every step of the way, and He continues to do so. Not everyone turns to faith to deal with their anger, but that is what made the difference in my life.

All of us have experienced anger. Some of us have cringed under the rage in our families, struggled with it in our souls, felt it toward our friends and loved ones. Some of us have shocked others with volcanoes of anger.

What Is Anger?

When you think about anger, what words or pictures come to mind? Frustration? Rage?

- 23% of Americans admit they openly express their anger.

- 39% say they hold it in or hide it.

- 23% say they walk away from the situation.

- 23% confess to having hit someone in anger.

- 17% admit they have destroyed the property of someone who made them mad.

Anger can be defined as an aversive state ranging from annoyance to rage. Webster's says, "Anger is a strong feeling of displeasure and antagonism, indignation or an automatic reaction to any real or imagined insult, frustration, or injustice, producing emotional agitation seeking expression."

Let's look at the problem of anger in our society. Anger's effects are evident. There is rampant violence in schools, families, and neighborhoods.

For example: Severe violence is a chronic feature of 13% of all marriages and generally 35 violent incidents occur before any type of report is made. Every 25 seconds someone is a victim of a violent crime such as murder, robbery, assault or rape.

Anger is one of the most troubling emotions! We sometimes hear blatant admonishments such as "we shouldn't ever be angry." So what happens to our anger? We end up feeling guilty for being angry, or we pretend we're not angry, or we numb our feelings or turn our anger into depression.

"Frustration and anger are normal responses to many negative situations and problems we face in life. Often we have difficulty taking responsibility for and honestly expressing our anger. Sometimes guilt we feel as a result of being angry builds-- causing inner shame and turmoil. Hostility, aggression, resentment, hatred, rage may or may not be manifested or play a part in an angry episode."
R. Potter-Efron

What is Anger Management? Anger Management is the ability to recognize anger and develop and apply skills and abilities to respond in a healthy and socially appropriate manner. Anger management needs to include evidence-based treatment strategies.

Foundational Insights:
Anger is an energy or force which is often harmful. Anger is caused by feelings of helplessness and the need to control situations, people and consequences. Anger — when expressed in a healthy way — can foster personal growth and significance, improving relationships and changing lives.

Anger Management Worksheet

1. What might you be feeling underneath your anger? Describe the feelings here:

> Fear? ___
>
> Sadness? ___
>
> Frustration? ___
>
> Disappointment? ___
>
> Invalidated? ___
>
> Disrespected? ___
>
> Wronged? ___
>
> Helpless? ___
>
> Other? _____

2. What would happen if you were to express those feelings or thoughts to the other person? Identify the pros and cons for expressing your real feelings.

_____
_____
_____
_____

3. Write out a recent scenario when you felt angry. Explain the facts of the scenario and then, analyze what feelings (as above) were underneath and the reasons for those feelings.

_____
_____
_____
_____
_____
_____

4. List the reasons you are taking this course. List what you hope to learn:

___

What is your Biggest Anger Trap?

5. Do you agree or disagree with the Foundational Insights? What do these statements teach about the underlying reasons for anger?

___

6. Do you ever get angry? Write out one situation which generally makes you feel angry.

___

7. How would your life be different if you were to respond to anger in a healthy way?

___

What would need to change?

___

8. How would you define anger?

What pictures or words come to mind when you think of anger?

_____
_____
_____
_____

9. How have you experienced anger in your family? Can you identify with Ted and/or Lynette?

_____
_____
_____
_____
_____

10. How do you generally express your anger? Write out the consequences of your anger:

_____
_____
_____
_____
_____
_____

11. When have you expressed your anger or frustration in a healthy way? What was the result?

_____
_____
_____
_____

12. If you could wake up tomorrow and manage your anger – what would be different?

_____
_____
_____

Project:
You are a reporter for a newspaper. Write a short article on:
"Anger in the 21st century: triggers and consequences for teen anger."
Post it on your web space or profile. Share it with your group or mentor.

*GLOSSARY

Aggression- Behavior intended to cause psychological or physical harm to someone or to a surrogate target. The behavior may be verbal or physical, direct or indirect.

Anger- A negatively toned emotion, subjectively experienced as an aroused state of antagonism toward someone or something perceived to be the source of an aversive event.

Anger control- The regulation of anger activation and its intensity, duration, and mode of expression. Regulation occurs through cognitive, somatic, and behavioral systems.

Anger reactivity- Responding to aversive, threatening, or other stressful stimuli with anger reactions characterized by automaticity of engagement, high intensity, and short latency.

Escalation of provocation- Incremental increases in the probability of anger and aggression, occurring as reciprocally heightened antagonism in an interpersonal exchange.

Frustration- Either a situational blocking or impeding of behavior toward a goal or the subjective feeling of being thwarted in attempting to reach a goal.

Hostility- An attitudinal disposition of antagonism toward another person or social system. It represents a predisposition to respond with aggression under conditions of perceived threat.

Inhibition- A restraining influence on anger expression. The restraint may be associated with either external or internal factors.

Rage- The strongest form of anger, very physical, threatening the other individual with possible lack of control over actions.

Violence- Seriously injurious aggressive behavior, typically having some larger societal significance. The injury may be immediate or delayed.

Resource: Raymond W. Novaco. Encyclopedia of Psychotherapy, VOLUME 1, Copyright 2002, Elsevier Science (USA).

Hatred- The end product of the resentment process. Hatred is "frozen" anger that results in an intense and unchanging dislike of another.

Lesson Two: The Power of Anger

Goals: Identify the process of anger, how anger can be helpful and how it is harmful. Normalize anger and identify triggers provoking anger.

Anger is a great force. If you control it -- it can be transmuted into a power which can move the whole world.

William Shenstone

Anger can actually be helpful. Anger is like a warning signal alerting you that something is wrong. It can provide the energy to resist emotional or physical threats. Anger can help you mobilize your resources and set appropriate limits and boundaries. Your anger can give you strength to resist threatening demands or a violation of your values.

Anger helps you overcome the fear of asserting your needs and facing conflict. Anger can be used for beneficial purposes.

And yes, anger can be harmful. As Will Rogers quipped, "People who fly into a rage always make a bad landing." William Blake wrote: *"I was angry with my friend. I told my wrath, my wrath did end. I was angry with my foe; I told it not, my wrath did grow."*

Unexpressed anger is not only harmful to you physically, but it plays havoc on your emotions and your spirituality. When you don't talk about your anger and the issue that upsets you, you are pretending that everything is fine and are hiding your true feelings. You end up living a lie. The Good Book says, "having put away falsehood, let each one of you speak the truth with his neighbor, for we are members one of another." [1]

Harmful anger costs you too much physically. It yields the largest increases in heart rate and blood pressure of all emotional reactions. Anger results in ulcers, cardiovascular diseases, colitis, and a depleted immune system. Not only is it damaging to the body, but anger damages mental health and relationships.

Signs indicating when anger is a problem:
- When it is too frequent.
- When it is too intense.
- When it lasts too long.
- When it leads to aggression.
- When it disturbs school, work or relationships.

When Anger Wakes Up

To help you understand why it is hard to shake anger after it wakes up, you need to learn the physiological mechanism involved in anger arousal:

When you perceive a threat or provocation, your internal fight/flight response is alerted. Within less than a second breathing and heart rate increases. Then a hormonal surge kicks in that lasts thirty minutes. Your long-term anger response can be abbreviated when the early stage of anger arousal is interrupted.

Who's responsible for your anger? People often blame others for their anger or situations which are stressful. But, the truth is -- you make the decision to get angry. No one can control you and your feelings. People may try to make you mad, but you make a choice about whether to get angry, laugh, work through the issue or forget about it.

Anger Triggers
Factors that can impact anger arousal in individuals include the following: Undesirable bodily states actually can increase anger arousal. Fatigue, sleep deprivation, pain, hangovers all lower the threshold of reactivity to an event that can precipitate anger. Premenstrual syndrome and low blood sugar can actually contribute to aggression.
High intakes of sugar trigger a surge of insulin that not only converts sugar just consumed but also other available sugar. This leads to depressed blood sugar levels, resulting in moodiness and triggering irritability and aggression.

Cognitive triggers: The way you perceive an event determines the extent to which you judge it as threatening provocation. Extremely rigid or biased appraisals of events prime you for over-reaction to what might normally be only a slightly irritating incident.
How you create anger:

Anger cycle #1 begins with an event or some stress that leads to Trigger Thoughts:

These cycles are self-perpetuating. Your self-talk can keep your anger simmering.
Here's an example for *anger cycle #1:* A friend stands you up for a luncheon date, and you begin to think about how this friend has let you down in the past. This triggers hurt and anger and more thoughts about how this friend's behavior has disappointed you, which results in more anger.

Anger cycle #2: Another way to arouse anger is by Trigger Thoughts that actually create some arousal or stress. This results in feelings of anger, which leads to more Trigger Thoughts, creating a stress reaction that fuels more anger.

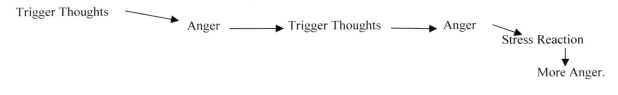

Here's an example for *anger cycle #2*: Arturo wonders if his friend will stay late after school. He imagines himself waiting to play basketball in the gym. These thoughts trigger a sense of disappointment and frustration. He thinks the pain is his friend's fault and converts his stressful feelings to anger. This stirs up more Trigger Thoughts as he tells himself, "He's so forgetful."

Other sources that may trigger your anger include *biases*. For example, you may favor certain types of inputs or interpretations of events over others. A bias leads you to interpret an event as aversive or negative. Thus you may perceive an accidental bump in the school hallway as premeditated. This kind of appraisal system makes too much of provoking events, triggering anger.

Another common bias is: "If you provoke me, it is OK for me to strike back." This type of thinking sets the stage for retaliation. A final type of misappraisal system can be called the "knuckle bias." As one adolescent put it, "The only thing they'll understand is a fist in the face." This kind of bias leads you to believe that aggressive force is the only option that has any meaningful effect. Many people today think that violence is an acceptable way to settle disputes.

Irrational Beliefs
While biases affect how input is weighed, generalized beliefs that you may hold will see provoking input even when there is no intentional provocation. You may think that people must or should act in a certain way and when they fail to meet these standards, you get angry. (McKay et al., 1988)

Common anger-inducing beliefs include:
- Because I want it, I should get it (entitlement). "They should appreciate my work." "I should get . . ."
- It has to be fair. "Since I worked as hard as she did, I should . . ."
- I have to be right (self-righteousness). "No, it's not that way, it's . . ." "I just don't think that's right."
- "If you cared about me, you . . ." (conditional assumption). "If I was important to you, you'd . . ." "If you were my friend, you'd . . ."
- I have to be in control. (This frequently underlies jealousy.) "Are you going out dressed that way?" "I'm not leaving until you . . ."

(Gintner, 1995, p. 9.)

The important aspect about irrational beliefs is that you really believe there is a good reason for getting upset. You feel threatened and fear that something awful may happen, even when the event is minor. Or you may be dealing with low self-esteem, which can cause an overreaction to events.

Impulsivity is frequently attributed to an underdeveloped defensive system. This is seen in adolescence more often than in mature adults. Defenses like sublimation (which refocuses energy into positive behavior) or rationalization (which constructs a logical justification for someone's actions) are unavailable for delaying an anger response. The impulsive person rarely quells a horrible urge by a rationalization such as "He's probably having a bad day." Rather, immature defenses such as fantasy, denial, or acting out are the major emotional regulators. Anger explosions operate like a release valve so that "you act it out" instead of "thinking it out."

Skill deficits in cognitive and behavioral areas contribute to an impulsive acting out of anger. There are ways to avoid or escape this. One way is using self-talk to guide behavior and delay responses (for example, "Wait a minute--hitting won't help right now. Take a breather").
Those with poor self-control are characterized by hot self-talk: "He thinks he can bully me . . ." Or the person ruminates about events, allowing the anger to build internally. Those with healthy self-talk think, "I'm not going to think about that now. I'm going to get some work done   ." or entertain alternative solutions to provocation such as problem-solving.

Substance use: This addictive/obsessive behavior has a disinhibiting effect on anger and on aggression. Thus the person speaks or acts in ways that normally he/she would not even consider.

Family: An aggressive individual typically comes out of a home environment characterized by high overt conflict and low levels of positive interchanges.

Stress--current life situations: Living under conditions of chronic stress, or frequent daily hassles, takes a toll on an individual's coping resources.
A major stressful life event (such as divorce or death) on top of chronic stress (such as harsh economic conditions and unemployment) can lead to an aggressive overreaction.
Example: marital discord resulting in child abuse.
Consider media reports of those who go on a murder spree after a job loss or marital separation. Who or what is responsible? The person who is angry and acts out his/her anger is responsible.

What Happens in the Process of Anger?
When someone hurts us physically or emotionally we become angry. We may flare up immediately or think about it awhile and then become angry. Something happens when we are frustrated: someone or something prevents us from reaching a goal. The anger covers up our feelings of disappointment or failure. In the short run it may keep us going. In the long run it will deplete our emotional energy. Poor self-concept, negative self-evaluations and fear lie behind the anger.

Dr. Paul Hauck outlines six levels of thought people move through in getting angry:
1. "I want something."
2. "I didn't get what I wanted and am frustrated."
3. "It is awful and terrible not to get what I want."
4. "You shouldn't frustrate me! I must have my way."
5. "You're bad for frustrating me."
6. "Bad people ought to be punished."

Apply these steps to a recent episode in which you became angry. Our perception of truth begins to break down in level 3. We don't like to be frustrated, but being frustrated is not as terrible as we think. Levels 4-6 show a retreat to irrationality and can result in uncontrolled anger as we think these unhealthy thoughts.

Why must we have our way? Who says people are bad just because they frustrate us? Who says bad people ought to be punished? What is involved at the level of thought when anger goes bad? Cognitive distortions; irrational beliefs; false beliefs about spiritual truth, what is good for us, and how we can or cannot secure significance.

Foundational Insights:
Anger is a response to fear, helplessness, frustrated goals, tense or difficult situations, false beliefs, conflicts, or stress. Triggers can increase an angry response. But when the situation or event is analyzed, one should determine whether there is a legitimate reason for getting angry. Maybe it is: "I don't like the decision that was made because_____." Or "I felt disrespected or misjudged by the way I was treated." The key is to identify the issue and decide whether it is valid. Then approach the situation or person to work through the matter in a healthy way.

Questions for Thought

1. How would you describe anger?
   Anger is:
   Anger reminds me of:
   Anger is another word for:
   Anger makes me feel:
   Anger sounds like:

   _____
   _____
   _____

2. When have you been angry and discovered later there was no legitimate reason for your response?
   _____
   _____

3. What triggered the anger?
   _____
   _____

4. What were your feelings/thoughts beneath the anger? Disappointment, fear, frustration, loneliness, hopelessness, helplessness, inferiority?
   _____
   _____

5. When did you get angry over a legitimate issue? What was the issue?

_____
_____
_____
_____

Were you able to work through it effectively without harming the other person or yourself?

_____
_____

6. Take the following Irrational Belief Inventory. Check which belief(s) applies to you:

I regularly think:

    ___Because I want it, I should get it (entitlement). "They should appreciate my work." "I should get . . ."
    ___It has to be fair. "Since I worked as hard as she did, I should .. ."
    ___I have to be right (self-righteousness). "No, it's not that way, it's . . ." "I just don't think that's right."
    ___"If you cared about me, you . . ." (conditional assumption). "If I was important to you, you'd . . ." "If you were my friend, you'd . . ."
    ___I have to be in control. (This frequently underlies jealousy.) "Are you going out dressed that way?" "I'm not leaving until you . . ."   (Gintner)

Which belief(s) do you struggle with? How much do these beliefs inhibit anger control?

_____
_____

7. What are some sources of and triggers for anger described in the book?

_____
_____

8. What happens in the process of anger according to the book?

_____
_____
_____

"Anger can actually be helpful.
    Anger is like a warning signal alerting you that something is wrong. It can provide the energy to resist emotional or physical threats. Anger can help you mobilize your resources and set appropriate limits and boundaries. Your anger can give you strength to resist threatening demands or a violation of your values." (What's Good About Anger?)

9. When can anger be helpful according to the book? Do you agree or disagree?
_____
_____
_____
_____

"Harmful anger costs you too much physically. It yields the largest increases in heart rate and blood pressure of all emotional reactions. Anger results in ulcers, cardiovascular diseases, colitis, and a depleted immune system. Not only is it damaging to the body, but anger damages mental health and relationships." (What's Good About Anger?)

10. When can anger be harmful according to the authors? Would you add any harmful effects to the list?
_____
_____
_____
_____

11. Who is responsible for getting angry? Do you tend to blame others for your anger?
_____
_____

12. Check which of the following signs of problem anger apply to you:
    1. It is too frequent. ___ : I get really angry 2-3 times a day.
    2. It is too intense. ___ : My anger causes me to explode or become resentful
    3. It lasts too long. ___ : I can't let anger go. I think about it most of the time.
    4. It leads to aggression. ___ : I lash out – hitting things or hurting myself or others.
    5. It disturbs school, work or relationships. ___ : I can't concentrate at work or school or have healthy relationships.

13. What might you be doing to contribute to your anger?
_____
_____

Check which *Aversive bodily states* apply to you:
1. Fatigue
2. Sleep deprivation
3. Pain
4. Hangovers
5. PMS/hormonal changes
6. High/Low blood sugar

What about the following?
Cognitive triggers: Do you see events and people as threatening your goals most of the time? Do you overreact to what others would consider—slightly irritating incidents?

Can you identify with any of these triggers? Circle and describe:
      a. Irrational beliefs
      b. Biases
      c. Skill deficits
      d. Use drugs or alcohol
      e. Stress overload

14. How has your family played a role in the way that you now handle your anger?

___

> **Which Triggers cause you to fall into the Anger Trap?**

___

Anger Survey:

15. Review the survey: In what kinds of situations do you find yourself getting angry?

How has anger been a problem for you?

What triggers or causes did you discover led to feelings of anger/frustration?

What if Question:

16. *What if you are at school and another student starts 'getting in your face' about not keeping up with a project?*

Your anger quotient is: 1-10 (1=low; 5= moderate; 10=high) _____

What are any triggers?
_____
_____

Your response is:
_____
_____
_____

What's good about your response (thoughts, behavior)?
_____
_____

Describe the consequences of your real response:
_____
_____

How does this help you achieve your goals?
_____
_____

What do you need to change for better results (instead of fights or trouble with school authorities)?
_____
_____

Assignment: Write out a recent General Provocation Scenario from your own life. Keep a daily log of your anger. Complete the Anger Management Report weekly.

What are your Anger Survey results now from pg. 8? (circle one):

Category I   Category II   Category III

Please measure your use of anger coping skills from 1-10: _____
(1=poor use of skills   5=intermittent use of skills   10=consistent use of skills)

Lesson Three: What IS Good About Anger?

Goal: To learn how anger can be expressed in healthy ways to achieve your goals.

There is good anger. It is anger governed by self-control, motivated by compassion, desiring what is right versus what is wrong.

Lynette Hoy

Do you struggle with the question, "How can anything good come from anger?" You are not alone. While there are plenty of examples of harmful anger, we rarely encounter good examples.

How many times this week did you get angry? Highlight the kind of behavior that resulted:
- yelling
- rude or obscene remarks
- aggression, violence
- depression, hidden anger
- other _____

What were the consequences? Highlight the attitudes or consequences that resulted:
- sense of guilt, regret, or shame
- defensiveness or thinking, "They deserved it"
- more anger, resentment
- broken relationships
- trouble with the law or your teacher (or employer)

The premise of this book is that feelings of anger are normal and at times justified. The degree to which you become angry, the reasons for your anger, and the outcome of your anger determine whether your anger is, in fact, good. When anger is expressed in healthy ways, it is a change agent. Anger can actually change a passive victim into someone who is confident and assertive. An aggressive person can learn self-control. Anger can motivate people to solve problems and resolve conflict.

Your anger can be converted into forgiveness versus internalized as resentment.

But when anger is hidden and suppressed, it most likely will result in depression. The tendency for many religious people and leaders is to avoid the expression of anger because they believe anger is wrong in any situation. Thus anger is viewed negatively and is often denied.

In the following situation Bob writes about his struggles with anger and control:

"My anger always stayed in check at school. One day I was tested beyond imagination by a classmate who was trying to pick a fight over who was right regarding a particular situation.

I allowed someone to gain control over me by losing my temper and yelling in the middle of the school hallway. The ironic point is that my faulty thinking said anger equals control, and by getting angry I gave up that one thing in my mind that was worth fighting for: control.

The biggest cost was the alienation that followed. It isolated me from the very people to whom I wanted to be close. Instead of control, I gained loneliness."

Bob didn't get what he wanted. He also lost the respect and friendship of a close friend.

So, what is good about anger? Anger:
- gives you information about yourself, events, and people
- helps energize you for action and faith
- moves you to express your feelings and resolve conflict
- enables you to assert yourself and move toward problem-solving

What are some sensible, healthy admonitions for being "good and angry?"
1. Be angry, but put limitations on its expression in order to prevent harming yourself or others.
2. Take responsibility for your anger. Don't blame it on someone else.
3. Slow your anger down. Think through anger versus immediately acting it out. [1]
4. Don't let your anger intensify, as it will generally bring about harm.
5. Don't associate with angry people. [2]
6. Seek healthy resolution to issues.
7. Always consider the outcome of anger and how it will impact others as well as yourself.
8. Learn healthy ways to express your anger.

Here's How You Can Handle Someone Else's Anger-
We tend to get angry at someone who is angry. Why is that? We react defensively to angry people because we think their anger is wrong and threatening. What can we do to drain the anger from someone else versus provoking their anger even more?

King Solomon wrote, "a gentle answer turns away wrath, but a harsh word stirs up anger." [3]
A simple method of paraphrasing what an angry person says to you can help defuse his/her anger.

Here's an example:
Angry person: "I can't stand the stress of you interrupting me when I am working on a project. You are so inconsiderate!"
You say, "You find it very stressful when I interrupt you during an important project."
Angry person: "Yes! And furthermore, I need more peace and quiet around here."
You say, "You would like more peace and want me to stop interrupting you."
Angry person: "Yes. You seem to have gotten the message."
You say, "I appreciate you sharing this with me. In the future, I will try to avoid interrupting you when I see you concentrating on a project."
At a later time when the person's anger has subsided, bring up the other issues that need resolution by saying, "When would be a good time for me to discuss my questions and concerns with you in the future?" and/or "It would be helpful when you have a problem with my behavior to stick to the issue and not call me 'inconsiderate'."

This example of paraphrasing should generally be used for the purpose of defusing and draining someone else's anger. It is not sufficient for use in cases where you need to work through a conflict with someone or deal with an unfair accusation or an abusive situation.

The premise of this book is to teach you that anger is good when turned into:
- Faith: Trusting in your Higher Power
- Assertiveness: Speaking the truth in love
- Problem-solving: Seeking the best solution
- Conflict resolution: Negotiating to win-win
- Forgiveness: Letting go of resentment

What's in it for you?
What will you get out of controlling your anger? First of all, you will gain self-control and a sense of "personal power" (not power over others). No one will be able to make you angry or pull your strings. You will have the power to choose to be angry or not! Having "personal power" is pulling your own strings and gaining control over yourself. If you can keep cool, you are more likely to respond in ways that serve your best interests.

Look at the pros and cons of reacting to provocation with aggression. What are the positives and negatives?

If someone calls you a name and you hit him/her, you believe "they'll think twice about messing with me."

On the other hand, you may get sued or arrested for assault and battery. When you avoid responding aggressively, you gain self-respect and, most likely, respect from others. You also avoid negative consequences with the law.

Foundational Insights:
When we step back and assess the situations that cause us to feel angry, we can plan for a healthy response. When we consider the consequences for our response and the best interests of others and ourselves, we are motivated to express anger effectively and appropriately.

Questions for Thought

1. Do you really believe that not all anger is wrong, that in fact anger is sometimes good? Why or why not?
_____
_____
_____

2. What motivates you to change how you handle anger?
_____
_____
_____

What's Good About Anger? Expanded Book & Workbook for Teens

3. What impact will it have when you become aware of your intentions, goals, and outcomes regarding your anger?
_____
_____
_____

4. When have you considered how your anger will affect someone else?
_____
_____

5. What does it mean to have "personal power"? What are the pros and cons of keeping your cool and pulling your own strings? How does having "personal power" differ from control?
_____
_____
_____
_____

6. What have you learned from King Solomon's advice about responding to those who are angry? Do you agree or disagree?
_____
_____
_____
_____

7. Describe what this lesson means to you. In other words, *what is good about anger* and does this make sense to you?
_____
_____

8. How did Bob's anger get out of control at school? What were the consequences of his anger? Can you identify with Bob?
_____
_____
_____

9. State in your own words some of the admonitions for being "good and angry."
_____
_____
_____

10. How can you handle your parent's or friend's anger according to this lesson? Do you agree with this approach?
_____
_____

What limitations should be applied to the approach for handling someone else's anger?

11. Describe a situation when someone else was angry and how you responded:

12. What could you have done differently to help that person?

13. Describe the pros and cons for controlling your anger.

14. When you implement "personal power" -- what will you gain *from pulling your own strings*?

15. List three situations you would like to handle with more self-control and wisdom.

a.

b.

c.

What if Question:
16. *What if your friend interrupts you when you are trying to explain something very important?*

Your anger quotient is: 1-10 (1=low; 5= moderate; 10=high) _____

Your response is:
_____
_____
_____

What's good about your response (thoughts, behavior)?
_____
_____

Describe the consequences of your response:
_____
_____

How does this help you achieve your goals?
_____
_____

What do you need to change?
_____
_____

Assignment: Write out a recent General Provocation Scenario from your own life. Keep a daily log of your anger. Complete the Anger Management Report weekly.

What are your Anger Survey results now from pg.8? (circle one):

Category I   Category II   Category III

Please measure your use of anger coping skills from 1-10: _____
(1=poor use of skills; 5=intermittent use of skills; 10=consistent use of skills)

Lesson Four: Defusing Anger by Managing Stress

Goal: Identify and reduce stressors to enhance anger management.

There are very few certainties that touch us all in this mortal experience, but one of the absolutes is that we will experience hardship and stress at some point.

Dr. James Dobson

What role does stress play in anger escalation? Research has demonstrated that high stress levels precipitate angry outbursts and aggression. Take the stress inventory at the end of this lesson to learn how stress is impacting your life and emotions.

Overview of Stress: The Wikipedia Encyclopedia states that "Stress (roughly the opposite of relaxation) is a medical term for a wide range of strong external stimuli, both physiological and psychological, which can cause a physiological response called the general adaptation syndrome, first described in 1936 by Hans Selye in the Journal of Nature."

Stress and its effects

Selye was able to separate the physical effects of stress from other physical symptoms suffered by patients through his research. He observed that patients suffered physical effects not caused directly by their disease or by their medical condition.

Selye described the general adaptation syndrome as having three stages:
- alarm reaction, where the body detects the external stimulus.
- adaptation, where the body engages defensive countermeasures against the stressor.
- exhaustion, where the body begins to run out of defenses.

There are two types of stress: eustress ("positive stress") and distress ("negative stress"), roughly meaning challenge and overload.

Both types may be the result of negative or positive events. If a person both wins the lottery and has a beloved relative die on the same day, one event does not cancel the other -- both are stressful events. Eustress is essential to life, like exercise to a muscle; however, distress can cause disease. (Note that what causes distress for one person may cause eustress for another, depending upon each individual's life perception.) When the word stress is used alone, typically it is referring to distress. Serenity is defined as a state in which an individual is disposition-free or largely free from the negative effects of stress, and in some cultures it is considered a state that can be cultivated by various practices, such as meditation and other forms of training. Stress can directly and indirectly contribute to general or specific disorders of body and mind. Stress can have a major impact on the physical functioning of the human body. Such stress raises the level of adrenaline and corticosterone in the body, which in turn increases the heart rate, respiration, and blood pressure and puts more physical stress on bodily organs. Long-term stress can be a contributing factor in heart failure, high blood pressure, stroke and other illnesses.

Stress is a threat to the safety and well-being of the body. In time past, the physical stress response was a means of survival: it prepared us for fight or flight. What is this so-called fight or flight reaction? It is instinctive and consists of messages sent all over the body to and from the brain. These messages alert the body of a perceived threat. In a threatening situation, we are given two options: either we can stand our ground and fight the threat or we can run away from it. The choice is made based on our perception of the situation: if we feel we have a chance of overcoming the danger (e.g., winning the fight) or not.

The various triggers for anger covered earlier are also triggers for a stress response. A stress reaction can precipitate or coincide with an angry response. Thus, avoiding triggers such as drinking, substance abuse, hot self-talk, irrational beliefs, distorted thoughts, overspending, unhealthy behavior, and any preventable stressful situations can thwart angry responses. Obviously, there are stressful circumstances in life that cannot be avoided.

Changing what you say to yourself and how you view life can greatly impact how you manage stress and anger. Your self-talk originates from your view of life and yourself. If you view life as "grab for all the gusto you can get!" based on the premise that "eat, drink, and be merry, for tomorrow we die," then you will experience more stress and anger! Why? Because you will hurry through life looking for satisfaction in anything without thinking about the consequences or caring about what is best for your life and those you love. And you will experience dissatisfaction -- the opposite of what you really want! If you view life as meaningless, you will tell yourself, "what's the point?" or "why bother?" when you face responsibilities and decisions. Or if you view life as overwhelming or yourself as never measuring up, you will tell yourself, "I can't handle that" or "This is too much for me" or "I'll just fail anyway." Your negative self-talk will generate more feelings of stress, hopelessness, and less motivation for change. We call this inner talk "stress-talk." Stress-talk will cause more anger and frustration in your life. The lessons on cognitive distortions can help you challenge and change any stress-talk.

Other internal stress-talk messages occur when you try to control people. You may say to yourself, "He/she should do it my way" or "Why is she/he not doing things my way?" because of your need to control. Underlying your need to control may be feelings of insecurity, jealousy, low self-worth, or the urge to teach others how to live their lives. Whatever the cause, your need for control will increase your feelings of stress and anger.

How can you deal with the need to control? First, consider these negative consequences:
- You will run out of energy and feel more frustration when you try to control everything and everyone in your life.
- You will push your family and friends away from you. No one likes a controller.
- Generally, you won't get what you want when you try to control.
- In the long-run, your inner needs of security and significance won't be met.

Complete the Am I a Controller? inventory at the end of this lesson to see if you have this tendency.

Another form of stress-talk is blaming. You may be blaming others for your anger and disappointments in life, thinking, "if they would meet my needs I would be happy." The fact is that no one will completely meet your needs and that you have the power to make choices that will help fulfill your needs. You can take ownership of your feelings and better communicate your needs by saying to others:
"I feel angry (frustrated, disappointed, overwhelmed, hurt, or let down, etc.) when
you don't listen to me (or interrupt me)."
This formula for communication helps you express your reaction and emotions without blaming. It brings up the issue and helps the other person feel less defensive. Think about some situations when you could have used this formula:
    Situation:
    I felt angry when I thought:
    Identify the issue: Was it valid? Could you have made a request?

Balance your relationships and life in order to manage stress. We were made to connect with people. Having healthy, caring, significant relationships with others gives us meaning for living, encouragement, and companionship throughout our lives.
If you are in relationships that are unhealthy because you are giving more than getting or there is too much conflict and friction, then you will feel stressed out. It could be that you tend to be codependent and need boundaries or more assertiveness in your relationships.

What about focusing on your needs and preventing negative consequences? When you engage in activities that are unhealthy it increases stress and anger. You may think that you are managing your stress by drinking, smoking, or using other substances when actually these habits are making your life miserable. Substance abuse increases irritability and is a trigger for anger.
You need to decide what to change and how to make healthy choices that will improve your health, mind, emotions, spirit, and relationships. You may find comfort in the use of substances, but it will only be temporary. The long-term negative consequences will outweigh the short-term experience and increase feelings of anger.

How can you increase the eustress (positive stress) in your life?
Take a look at your life to see how you can get revitalized. Do you have some activities that encourage and inspire you such as exercise, singing, playing an instrument, going to church, involvement in a support group, or something else meaningful or creative?

Beginning a new goal such as a class or a hobby or sport will revitalize you. What past activities would you like to reestablish? Riding your bike? Going fishing? Taking an art class? Going hiking or canoeing? These kinds of activities will create "positive stress" and refresh you! Examine your personal pace of life. See what you might need to change. Simplify your life by starting to do and be that for which you were designed. You will begin to feel more hopeful, more peaceful and encouraged as you renew your whole person, soul, and spirit. Write out new goals for your life that will include the positive activities mentioned. Begin to do one or two activities daily that will help enrich you physically, emotionally, and spiritually. If you are interested in reading more about how faith affects anger, order the first edition of What's Good About Anger? or the DVD at: www.whatsgoodaboutanger.com

Progressive Relaxation
It has been proven that relaxation techniques are beneficial for reducing stress in your life and thus decreasing the resulting feelings of anger and frustration. With so many things to do, it's easy to put off taking time to relax each day. But in doing so, you miss out on the health benefits of relaxation. Relaxation can improve how your body responds to stress by:
- Slowing your heart rate, meaning less work for your heart.
- Reducing blood pressure.
- Slowing your breathing rate.
- Reducing the need for oxygen.
- Increasing blood flow to the major muscles.
- Lessening muscle tension.

After practicing relaxation skills, you may experience these benefits:
- Fewer symptoms of illness, such as headaches, nausea, diarrhea, and pain.
- Few emotional responses such as anger, crying, anxiety, apprehension, and frustration.
- More energy.
- Improved concentration.
- Greater ability to handle problems.
- More efficiency in daily activities.

Relaxed breathing
Have you ever noticed how you breathe when you're stressed? Stress typically causes rapid, shallow breathing. This kind of breathing sustains other aspects of the stress response, such as rapid heart rate and perspiration. If you can get control of your breathing, the spiraling effects of acute stress will automatically become less intense. Relaxed breathing, also called diaphragmatic breathing, can help you.

Practice this basic technique twice a day, every day, whenever you feel tense. Follow these steps:
1. Inhale. With your mouth closed and your shoulders relaxed, inhale as slowly and deeply as you can to the count of six. As you do that, push your stomach out. Allow the air to fill your diaphragm.
2. Hold. Keep the air in your lungs as you slowly count to four.
3. Exhale. Release the air through your mouth as you slowly count to six.
4. Repeat. Complete the inhale-hold-exhale cycle three to five times.

Recommended Relaxation Technique:
Experts say it's best to practice relaxation for at least twenty minutes per day. At first, practicing the following relaxation technique may seem awkward. In time, and with practice, you'll feel more comfortable with the practice and the results. Learning to relax can help prevent the escalation of anger.

Find a quiet place where you won't be disturbed. Make sure you're sitting comfortably with your back straight or lying comfortably with your arms along your sides. Close your eyes and begin focusing on your body. Slowly breathe in through your nose and out through your mouth.

When thoughts and images arise in your mind, acknowledge them, and then let them go away as you bring your focus back to your breathing. Fully experience each exhale. Practice this for about five minutes or so.

Shift your focus to your body. Start with your feet. Tighten the muscles in your feet and toes, hold them tense for a couple seconds, then release the tension and let your feet relax. Next, focus on your calves. Tighten the muscles in your calves, hold them tense for a couple seconds, then release the tension and let your calves relax.
Repeat this through all of your major muscle groups as you move your attention up your body. Tense your thighs, hold, and then relax.

Move to your chest, hands, arms, shoulders, and finally your face.
After you have relaxed all of your muscle groups, mentally check over your body from head to toe and feel for any muscles that are still tense. If you notice a part of you that is not totally relaxed, tense it up a little, hold, and then relax. Sit, or lay, in silence with your eyes closed for twenty minutes or for as long as is comfortable.
Many people incorporate prayer during their time of relaxation.

Foundational Insights:
Making personal choices to live a healthy life-style can decrease the stress that precipitates anger. Learning relaxation techniques can slow down your physiological "fight-flight" response to anger.

Which Stressors cause you to fall into the Anger Trap?

Questions for Thought

1. Take the stress inventory at the end of this lesson. What did you find out about your stress level? Which of the suggestions in this lesson could help you decrease the stress and anger in your life? Why? How can you apply the recommendations to your life? (Be practical.)
_____
_____
_____

2. What kind of "stress-talk" you struggle with? "Eat, drink and be merry, for tomorrow we die." "I can't handle that." "I'll just fail anyway." "He/she should do it my way."
"If he/she would meet my needs, I would be happy." Other:
_____
_____

3. How do you communicate your needs to others? Do you tend to blame or take ownership for your needs? What steps can you take to meet your own needs and responsibilities?
___
___
___

4. What happened when you tried the relaxation technique? How did you feel during and afterward?
___
___

5. What other types of activities help promote relaxation for you? Listening to music? Reading?
___
___

6. Ask yourself about your need to control and take the inventory. What about trying for the next two weeks to let those you have been trying to control make their own choices?
___
___

What if Question:
7. *What if your parent tells someone else something you shared with him/her in confidence?*

Your anger quotient is: 1-10 (1=low; 5= moderate; 10=high) _____
Your response is:
___
___
___

What's good about your response (thoughts, behavior)?
___
___

Describe the consequences of your response:
___
___

How does this help you achieve your goals?
___
___

What do you need to change? How could the stress management skills help your response?
___

Do You Fit the Description of a Controller or Abuser? Answer these questions honestly:

Do you ever do the following to a close friend or family member?
___ Embarrass, make sarcastic remarks or fun of him/her in front of your friends or family?
___ Put down his/her accomplishments or goals? Demonstrate extreme jealousy?
___ Make him/her feel unable to make decisions? Yell at her/him, let your temper get out of control?
___ Use intimidation or threats to gain compliance from her/him? Tell her/him that she/he is nothing without you?
___ Treat him/her roughly-grab, push, pinch, shove, or hit him/her?
___ Call her/him several times a night or show up to make sure she/he is where she/he said she/he would be?
___ Use drugs or alcohol as an excuse for saying hurtful things or abusing her/him?
___ Blame her/him for how you feel or act?
___ Pressure him/her sexually? Show cruelty to animals?
___ Make her/him feel like there is "no way out" of the relationship?
___ Prevent her/him from doing things she/he wants-like spending time with her/his friends or family?
___ Try to keep her/him from leaving after a fight or leave her/him somewhere after a fight to "teach her/him a lesson"?

Do you almost always need (with your close friends or relatives):
___ To have things done your way?
___ To have the last word?
___ To make your point understood?
___ To behave negatively (yell, use obscenities, put-downs, or name calling or force) when you don't get your way?
___ To behave negatively when you feel misunderstood?
___ To demonstrate how right you are?
___ To show how wrong he/she is?
___ To have your wishes granted?
___ To react negatively when he/she disappoints you?
___ To respond with an outburst of anger when he/she misunderstands or disappoints you?

Do you cause your friend/relative to:
___ Sometimes feel scared of you because you make threatening gestures or indirect threats or throw or break objects?
___ Make excuses for your behavior?
___ Believe that he/she is the only one who needs to change, not you?

___ Avoid conflict and never disagree with you in order to "keep the peace"?
___ Feel like no matter what he/she does, he/she can't please you?
___ Placate you by doing whatever you want and rarely doing what he/she wants?
___ Stay with you because he/she is afraid of the consequences of leaving you?

If you have checked any of these symptoms, you have the characteristics of a controller. If you checked any of these symptoms--physical, sexual abuse, verbal threats, outbursts or rageful behavior, harassment, manipulation by fear, cruelty to animals--you fit the description of a batterer and abuser with severe anger and control issues. You need help.

Explore these questions and challenge yourself: What makes you need to force someone to grant your every wish and expectation? You need to explore what is driving you to control and/or abuse him/her. Call a professional counselor. Contact a local domestic violence agency for Batterer's Intervention classes (in the USA, National Domestic Violence Agency at 1-800-799-7233).

For more resources visit www.counselcareconnection.org and www.whatsgoodaboutanger.com

THE STRESS OF ADJUSTING TO CHANGE

EVENTS	SCALE OF IMPACT
Death of a significant other	100
Abortion	100
Divorce (of parents)	73
Marital separation (of parents)	65
Jail term	63
Death of close family member	63
Personal injury or illness	53
Marriage (of parent)	50
Suspended from school	47
Marital reconciliation (of parents)	45
Change in health of family member	44
Pregnancy	40
Sexual promiscuity/STDs	39
Gain of new family member	39
School readjustment	39
Change in financial state	38
Death of close friend	37
Change to different school/work	36
Change in number of arguments with close friend/family member	35
School loan	31
Foreclosure of mortgage or loan	30
Change in responsibilities at school/work	29
Family member leaving home	29
Trouble with family members	29
Outstanding personal achievement	28
Parent begins or stops work	26
Begin or end school	26
Change in living conditions	25
Revision of personal habits	24
Trouble with teacher/parent/boss	23
Change in school/work hours or conditions	20
Change in residence	20
Change in schools	20
Change in recreation	19
Change in church activities	19
Change in social activities	18
Change in sleeping habits	16
Change in number of family gatherings	15
Change in eating habits	15
Vacation	13
Christmas	12
Minor violations of the law	11
Total:	____

Determine which life events have occurred in your life over the past two years and add up your total stress score. If your total score is under 150, you are less likely to be suffering the effects of cumulative stress. If it is between 150 and 300, you may be suffering from chronic stress, depending on how you perceived and coped with the particular life events that occurred. If your score is over 300, it is likely you are experiencing some detrimental effects of cumulative stress. Please note that the degree to which any particular event is stressful to you will depend on how you perceive it. ***Resource: 1967, by Pergamon Press, Inc***

Assignment: Write out a recent General Provocation Scenario from your own life. Keep a daily log of your anger. Complete the Anger Management Report weekly.

What are your Anger Survey results now? (circle one):

Category 1   Category 11   Category 111

Please measure your use of anger coping skills from 1-10: _____
(1=poor use of skills; 5=intermittent use of skills; 10=consistent use of skills)

Lesson Five: Handling Anger Effectively

Goal: To learn how to process anger and frustration through healthy communication and problem-solving skills.

Anyone can become angry. That is easy. But to be angry with the right person, to the right degree, at the right time, for the right purpose and in the right way – that is not easy.

Aristotle

When you are overcome with anger, you may think it's impossible to have self-control. Let's take a look at some examples of people who experienced being "good and angry." Bob wrote the following in answer to the question, "How did you recently control your anger?"

"I stopped the cycle. When I missed seeing the trigger setup early enough to just avoid the trap, I still know what I feel like when I am starting to get angry. When I start to feel even a little like that, I just call for a time-out or I pause and remind myself of how important it is to remain in control of myself, not the other person.

"Recently I was having an emotionally charged discussion with my girlfriend. This of course means that we both felt strongly about the topic and had opposing viewpoints. I was able to look ahead and see how the conversation was going to unfold, so I stopped talking.
I started asking questions to understand her viewpoint. This is much easier to do when I remind myself that she is not trying to hurt me, she really cares about me, and she wants the best for both of us. It's amazing what some corrected thinking can accomplish."

Notice how this student applies a time-out, uses clarifying questions, corrects his thinking, and considers the potential escalation. These steps and skills keep anger and conflict from escalating. This is a healthy example of how to work through anger.

Many centuries ago a righteous man named Nehemiah wrote about an incident when he became angry: "I was very angry when I heard their outcry and these words. I took counsel with myself, and I brought charges against the nobles and the officials. I said to them, 'You are exacting interest, each from his brother.' And I held a great assembly against them." [1]
Nehemiah felt "very angry" when he heard about his country-men's dilemma (they were being exploited by the rich). He took time out to ponder the situation and how to approach it. He then went on to confront the nobles and officials. We see here that not all anger is wrong; there is a righteous anger, and it would be wrong not to act on it. As Aristotle said, "Anyone can become angry. That is easy. But to be angry with the right person, to the right degree, at the right time, for the right purpose and in the right way--that is not easy." What is the right way to handle anger? Here are some steps to consider.

Initial Awareness of Hurt or Anger

Too often we become extremely angry before we even recognize that we are angry. Early awareness is key. What are the elements of such early awareness?

1. Recognize the underlying feelings of tension, sadness, fear, frustration, hurt, rejection, etc.
2. Take time out to reflect. Be "slow to anger." [2]
3. Many find it helpful to pray about the problem, seeking spiritual help and guidance.
4. Identify the issue. Decide whether you are distorting the truth about the event or person.
What are you angry about?
What did the other person do that hurt or frustrated you? Think about the behavior that bothered you. Don't make judgments about others' motives.
5. Evaluate whether the issue is valid. Ask, "Do I have the right to be angry?" Sometimes we do, but sometimes we don't.
6. Address the issue/problem, and express your feelings: "I was frustrated/hurt/angry when you forgot about our appointment."
How are we to go about doing this?
• Establish a plan of action: "I would like to request that you call me the next time you are going to be late."
• Provide options for change: "Please take a break (time-out) when you begin to get angry." "Please treat me with respect."
• Negotiate a resolution: "What do you want to do about disciplining the children?"
• Plan a time-frame: "I would like to see changes made over the next month."
• Express how you will help the situation: "I will call a time-out if I think the conflict is getting too hot." "I will make my requests respectfully rather than nagging you in the future."
Learn to handle your anger with assertiveness (see the lesson on Anger and Assertiveness).
7. Get guidance from a pastor, counselor, or trustworthy confidante.
8. Put the issue in perspective. Ask yourself: "Is this issue really worth getting upset over and worth bringing up? Or can I let go of it in light of the fact that I may have misunderstood the person? Or maybe the issue/situation is just not that important and I can overlook it."
9. Forgive and forget. Forgiveness brings resolution and is a step toward reconciliation.

Problem-solving

Anger is a result of feeling that you are helpless in a given situation. You can't solve the problem. The problem is too big, overwhelming, or painful. Difficulties come in all sizes and shapes, and you seem to be having more than your fair share.
You may ask, "Why is life so difficult and hard? And why do some people seem to have it easy?"
Establish a plan of action. Write out options and solutions that will help you resolve the problem.

You would do well to consider the following:
• What can you learn about the issue you are facing?
• What can you do about this problem? List all reasonable options, and then choose one or two.
• Try out one of the options. You can always apply another option if your first choice is not working out. Evaluate how it is affecting you and others.
• How can someone help you? Ask for counsel.
• What resources are available to resolve your problem?
• What support can you ask for or make use of?

Thinking Ahead Reminders

Here are some ideas and questions to tell yourself before and during a conflict to maintain self-control:
> "Keep your breathing even."
> "What is it that I have to do?"
> "Take it one step at a time."
> "Stick to the issue and don't take it seriously."
> "What's going to happen if . . ."
> "Do I need to be cool so I'm not the fool?"
> "Is it really worth it?"
> "Will this make a difference in a week?"
> "What are some things I could say or do?"
> (Gintner, p. 22-23).

Write these down on a 3x5 card, then review and keep them in your wallet or purse.

Questions for Thought

1. Look back at a recent problem when you became angry.
Was the problem really a legitimate one? Was it worth discussing and trying to resolve?
___
___
___

2. Of the Thinking Ahead Reminders, which would help you cool down before or during a provoking situation?
___
___
___

3. What specific steps would you be willing to take (or have you taken) in the Handling Anger Effectively model to work through your anger?
___
___
___

4. Do the problem-solving steps make sense? When you face an issue, do you think, "What choices/options do I/we have?" or do you think, "It's my way or the highway?"
What needs to happen for you to become an "option-thinker?"
___
___
___

5. What skills and changes did Bob employ to help manage his anger when he was having an emotionally charged discussion with his girlfriend?
_____
_____

6. How would you evaluate one of your episodes of anger according to Aristotle's principles for being "good and angry" above?
_____
_____
_____

> # Which thoughts, people, expectations, hot self-talk or false beliefs cause you to fall into the ANGER TRAP?

Foundational Insights:
Anger may build inside when you feel invalidated or when you are unable to impact decisions or when you are frustrated in meeting personal and family needs and goals. Your anger may be based on unrealistic expectations of someone else or even yourself or an unhealthy need to control people and events. Identifying the validity of the issue underlying your anger and motivation is necessary to determine your plan of action or how to process the anger in effectively.

7. What are the causes of anger mentioned in this quote?
_____
_____

8. Write out the 9 steps for handling anger effectively.
_____
_____
_____
_____

9. What makes each step in the process so important?
_____
_____

10. Which steps have you implemented in the past? Which steps could help prevent an angry outburst in the future?

___

11. Identify the steps for problem-solving:

___

12. How can you apply some of these steps when a situation provokes you to anger in the future?

___

13. Which of the Thinking Ahead Reminders could help you "cool down" when facing an anger-provoking situation?

___

14. Do your angry episodes pass Aristotle's test for being "good and angry"? Why or why not?

___

What if Question:
15. *What if your teacher falsely accuses you of cheating on an exam?*

Your anger quotient is: 1-10 (1=low; 5= moderate; 10=high) _____

Your response is:

___

What's good about your response (thoughts, behavior)?

___

Describe the consequences of your response:

___

How does this help you achieve your goals?
_____
_____

What do you need to change? What skills could you apply from this lesson?
_____
_____

Assignment: Write out a recent General Provocation Scenario from your own life. Keep a daily log of your anger. Complete the Anger Management Report weekly.

What are your Anger Survey results now from pg. 8? (circle one):

Category 1   Category 11   Category 111

Please measure your use of anger coping skills from 1-10: _____
(1=poor use of skills; 5=intermittent use of skills; 10=consistent use of skills)

Lesson Six: Anger and Assertiveness

> **Goal:** To identify and apply ways of expressing anger and frustration through the use of assertive communication.

Do not be angry with me if I tell you the truth.

Socrates

Assertiveness is not aggressive or passive. Assertive people express their thoughts and feelings forthrightly without getting squashed or squashing others in the process.

Some who read this book might get the impression that one should never get angry--the risk is just too great. That, of course, is not the case. There are legitimate reasons for getting angry! Sometimes we rationalize and defend why we had an outburst. Other times we may try our hardest to not ever be angry.

Having your anger under control does not mean you have to be a wallflower--or, worse, a doormat--that you never disagree with anyone, never stand up for yourself, never confront someone and tell him or her that he or she is wrong. Handling anger the right way, with self-control, does not mean that you should stuff all angry feelings and never express them or be assertive.

Many people act out their anger aggressively, thinking they are just being assertive. The truth is that assertive behavior and communication are not aggressive, as we will explain later on. You may struggle with "acting out" your anger in harmful ways and thus, are experiencing legal, school, or relationship consequences. Making the choice to control the aggression and/or verbal outbursts will take determination and application of new behaviors and better ways to communicate.

Some of you may be indirect about expressing your feelings and needs. It's important to know that good anger is often assertive -- communicating reasonable requests and opinions.
Maybe you find this difficult. Perhaps as a child you were taught that it is self-centered to talk about yourself or to express your feelings. Or you may have grown up in a volatile environment where angry outbursts were the norm. Thus, you learned to react with "fits of rage" or out of fear--to hide your anger.

Which of the following describes your anger?

When I feel intense anger I have outbursts: ___

When I feel angry I lose my temper: ___

When I feel angry I tell the other person off: ___

When I feel angry I hide it and don't talk to the other person: ___

When I feel angry I use sarcasm to get my point across: ___

When I feel angry I ignore the problem but, feel resentful: ___

When I feel anger, I choose to distract myself: ___

When I feel anger, I find relief through drinking or use of substances: ___

*If you have checked any of the above-- learning assertive communication will help you! Take the assertiveness inventory at the end of this lesson.

You may not be direct about your opinions or disagreements because you fear people will be put off or that it will just cause a conflict. You may end up being so indirect that nearly all the time you let others speak for you. This type of communication tends to result in frustration and hidden anger.

As an indirect or passive person you may share your thoughts and feelings in a roundabout way and are apt to sound something like this: "They just laid off most of my department . . . It's kind of . . . . Well, you know. . . . But what can you do?" When you can't express your wants openly, you have to hint--"It looks like a nice day . . . our neighbors went to play tennis" or "The newspaper mentioned an arts and crafts show this Sunday"--and hope your friend will pick up on it.

You may be a person who doesn't give a hoot about what others think. You may give them the finger, shout, or threaten when they don't meet your expectations or cross you in some way.

You may struggle with "hot self-talk" and come out swinging when someone provokes you.

If you are non-assertive or passive it's difficult to decide when to stand up for your "reasonable rights" and state your opinion and when to go the extra mile in considering others' interests. You may end up apologizing for someone else's mistakes. When someone spills their coffee on you, you say you're sorry for being in the wrong place. When someone puts you down, you pretend you didn't hear the remark.

In either case, for those who are aggressive or passive, assertiveness is a healthy skill you can use effectively to defuse and work through anger.

A WORKING DEFINITION OF ASSERTIVENESS

What is assertiveness? It's a way of confronting an unpleasant or difficult situation without getting squashed or squashing others in the process. When you use assertiveness you can negotiate reasonable changes by stating directly what you think, feel, and want. Assertiveness builds intimacy, solves interpersonal problems, and increases honesty, valid requests, and legitimate refusals in your relationships. Assertiveness gives you the opportunity to air your grievances and frustrations in a healthy way instead of burying them or eventually blowing up.

Assertiveness is right!
I (Ted Griffin) can testify to the power and benefit of godly assertiveness, in this case my wife's. When I was tearing my family apart with selfish, destructive anger, my wife was able, with the courage God provides, to come to the point where she could at appropriate times tell me, "I won't allow you to talk to me in that way," then end the conversation until I had cooled down. Or she would leave the house, with the kids, leaving me alone at home to consider how my anger was affecting our family. In these and other ways her gentle but firm assertiveness made me see what my anger was doing to myself and to everyone in our home. Though I didn't always like her standing up to me at the time, looking back I can see that God used it to get my attention and to help me see how I was wrong and how I needed to change.

When I (Lynette) was first married, I would shut down and give the "cold shoulder" whenever I felt hurt by my husband. This brought a great deal of distress to our relationship because he could not understand what was wrong with me. One time he said, "Our relationship is more important than any issue. We need to work this out no matter what." It was obvious that I needed to learn how to directly communicate issues and any anger I was harboring in a healthier manner. Of course, there are a number of alternatives to healthy assertiveness. You can fake your feelings, suffer silently, retreat, manipulate, or demand your way in a fit of rage. Ultimately these options are self-defeating, harmful to you and others resulting in negative consequences.

PRACTICAL STRATEGIES FOR BEING APPROPRIATELY ASSERTIVE
One of the keys to making assertiveness work for you while also making it palatable for others is to combine it with active listening. Listening involves hearing and paraphrasing back what others say to you. It gives you the opportunity to pick up on their viewpoints and continue the dialogue. You don't have to agree with their opinions, but active listening will show that you value and respect them. This will increase the likelihood that others will take time to listen to you.

Begin summarizing what people say to you with phrases such as: • "In other words . . ."
- "Let me get this straight . . ."
- "So you felt that . . ."
- "What I hear you saying is . . ."
- "If I understand you correctly . . ."
- "Would you say that . . . ?"
- "Do I understand you to mean . . . ?"

Make certain that your paraphrase is brief and includes the facts and feelings the person is expressing. Some sample paraphrases might be:
- "You were really scared when the dog ran in front of the car."
- "You feel frustrated because I missed our appointment."

When you can summarize what someone has said to you, you will clarify what they are saying and keep the dialogue from getting heated.

Still, the most difficult aspect of communication comes when you take the risk to talk about your opinions, feelings, and needs. Don't let fear or anger get in the way! Learning assertive communication skills is the next step.

Here are some examples of ways of assertiveness that will help you express your opinions, confront others, state your feelings, or make requests:
1. Stating your preference or opinion: "My preference is _____."
   "What I'd like is _____."
2. Expressing your feelings: "I feel _____ when _____."
3. Making requests: "This movie is not what I hoped it would be. I would like to leave."
4. Disagreeing with someone: "I disagree with you when you say _____."
5. Saying yes or no without making excuses: "I am unable to come to lunch."
6. Using "I" statements for confronting: "I feel _____ when you _____ because _____."

Here is an assertiveness approach you can apply when you need to bring up an issue. It's called the ASERT Model:
- Approach the person calmly and with respect.
- State the problem. Think over and state the facts of the problem.
- Express yourself. State your feelings.
- Request change and feedback. Specify one behavior change.
- Then listen to the other person's thoughts and opinions.
- Talk it out. Paraphrase the other person's ideas. Discuss the consequences, considerations, and options.

Write out recent interactions you have had with people in which you could have been less demanding or less passive. Then, using the ASERT model, rewrite the scenario using the paraphrasing and assertiveness skills.

Resolve to start trying your newly acquired skills this week:
- When an acquaintance asks you for a favor that conflicts with your schedule, just say, "I wish I could help you, but I have another appointment."
- When you're standing in line and someone moves in front of you, say, "I believe I was first in line."
- When your friend owes you money--money you could use--say, "Would you please return the money you borrowed two weeks ago?"
- When you receive a bill that is unusually high for the service you received, ask for a refund or partial credit.
- When someone is rude to you, talk to them privately, asking them to treat you with respect in the future.
- When someone is talking about his or her opinions or beliefs, listen respectfully and then, freely share yours.

Assertiveness need not be a painful exercise of skills. You can get something out of communicating more directly with others. You can direct your anger into a healthy exchange of words leading to a resolution of problems. Aristotle wrote, "Many a friendship is lost for lack of speaking." Speaking up will help you build closer relationships with others and gain more confidence in yourself! Just think--no more hinting, raging, manipulating, forcing or demanding your way! Instead you can state your ideas, thoughts, and feelings confidently while at the same time managing your anger!

To be assertive in the ways we have been talking about is not easy. It takes wisdom (what to say and when to say it), patience, discernment, and above all courage.

Dealing with Difficult People: There are times when you will encounter people who are difficult and overbearing. Here are some suggestions for handling these situations.

1. *The broken record technique*: Rehearse making your requests in a firm but calm voice when someone does not respond to you. "I want my money back . . . just give me my money back . . . all I want is my money back . . ." It is critical to rehearse this prior to a situation in which you expect to encounter resistance and to help you maintain composure and self-control. Remember to not raise your voice.

2. When someone is engaging in annoying behavior, *"ignoring" or not reacting* may be the best course of action. Ignoring may lower the probability that it will occur again. However, this technique must be applied carefully since the other party may become more obnoxious. Ignoring includes: making no eye contact with the party and maintaining a neutral facial expression; attending to something else or the positive behaviors of the others in the room; as soon as the other party stops acting obnoxiously, attend to him/her.

3. *Fogging.* This technique is a way of confusing a provoking individual by appearing to lightheartedly agree with him or her. For example, a fogging response to someone who criticizes your clothing might be, "You really think I have no taste."
A fogging response helps you maintain control by not taking a comment seriously. It also breaks the escalation cycle by side-stepping an aggressive counter-response.
(Gintner; Feindler and Ecton)

Foundational Insights:
Anger can be communicated in acceptable and even loving ways. Anger can be expressed as a request, a boundary, an opinion, a decision or a question. When you communicate anger with respect – you will have more success in resolving issues, meeting your needs and building healthy relationships.

Questions for Thought

1. Did you find the working definition of assertiveness helpful or unrealistic? Why?
_____
_____
_____

2. Which of the Practical Strategies for Being Appropriately Assertive did you find most helpful? How can you implement this in your life?
_____
_____
_____

3. How can you use the ASERT Model effectively? Write out a situation(s) in which you will do this.
_____
_____
_____

4. How does the book describe assertiveness?
_____
_____
_____

5. How did you score on the assertiveness inventory? If you are an aggressive or volatile person when you get angry – how will learning assertive communication help you?
_____
_____

6. How can assertiveness help you better manage anger if you are a passive person or tend to hold your feelings in or are manipulative or indirect?
_____
_____
_____

7. What kind of assertiveness (making a request, stating a boundary or opinion, preference, decision or question) have you used in the past and how did it impact your anger?
_____
_____
_____
_____

8. Have you encountered difficult or over-bearing people? Describe one of the skills – broken record, ignoring, fogging – which will help you deal with these people/situations:
_____
_____
_____

9. **What if Question:**
What if you find out a friend said something cruel about you behind your back? Or what if your parent says you have to attend a family event which conflicts with plans you already had?

Your anger quotient is: 1-10 (1=low; 5= moderate; 10=high) _____

Your response is:
_____
_____

What's good about your response (thoughts, behavior)?
_____
_____

Describe the consequences of your response:
_____
_____
_____
_____

How does this help you achieve your goals?
_____
_____

What do you need to change? How could the ASERT approach help you respond?
_____
_____

Activity: Practice the Assertiveness scenarios found at the end of this book.

Additional Assignment: Write out examples of the times you have been appropriately assertive and discuss with your mentor or group:
_____
_____
_____
_____
_____
_____
_____
_____

Discuss and write out the pros and cons of being assertive here:
_____
_____
_____

Assignment: Write out a recent General Provocation Scenario from your own life. Keep a daily log of your anger. Complete the Anger Management Report weekly.

What are your Anger Survey results now from pg. 8? (circle one):

Category 1   Category 11   Category 111

Please measure your use of anger coping skills from 1-10: _____
(1=poor use of skills; 5=intermittent use of skills; 10=consistent use of skills)

What's Good About Anger? Expanded Book & Workbook for Teens

Assertiveness Inventory © copyright 2012 by Lynette J. Hoy, NCC, LCPC

This inventory will help you determine whether you are appropriately assertive, i.e., respectfully honest and direct about your feelings and opinions with others. Check the statements only if these are generally true of you. Be honest. This inventory may not be duplicated in any form.

When expressing myself I generally:
1. ___ have difficulty being clear and direct.
2. ___ keep quiet letting others speak.
3. ___ am abrasive or demanding.
4. ___ leave wishing I had said more.
5. ___ become too loud.
6. ___ say too much.
7. ___ clearly state how I feel or what I think.
8. ___ use active listening, tact and respect.
9. ___ ask others for their opinions after stating mine.
10. ___ tend to manipulate.
11. ___ make indirect suggestions about my feelings and thoughts.
12. ___ state my thoughts without denigrating someone's character.
13. ___ clarify what other people say.
14. ___ base my opinion on facts and behavior.
15. ___ label or stereotype others.
16. ___ consider others opinions as well as my own.
17. ___ find fault with other people.
18. ___ use a firm voice when necessary.
19. ___ use forceful gestures.
20. ___ communicate concern for others.
21. ___ quietly rationalize why I didn't speak up.
22. ___ hint about my feelings and wants.
23. ___ speak calmly and directly.
24. ___ turn conversations around to my needs and agenda.
25. ___ confront unpleasant issues directly but, with gentleness.
26. ___ when I am angry I tend to shut-down and give the "cold shoulder."
27. ___ when I am frustrated I don't hold back any of my feelings.
28. ___ I have difficulty communicating my ideas to others.

Once you have finished this inventory rate yourself as directed below.

Rate yourself as:
1. Appropriately assertive if you checked most of these:
7, 8, 9, 12, 13, 14, 16, 18, 20, 23, 25.
2. Passively pining if you checked any of these: 1, 2, 4, 21, 26, 28
3. Mostly manipulative if you checked: 10, 11, 22, 24
4. Aggressive or blaming if you checked: 3, 5, 6, 15, 17, 19, 27
5. Muddled mess: if you checked some of statements from more than one of the categories.

Lesson Seven: Managing Conflict

Goal: To identify and apply conflict resolution skills to disputes and disagreements.

I don't have to attend every argument I'm invited to.

Author Unknown

Whenever you are angry, you are dealing with conflict as well; and every time you experience real conflict, you also, at least to some extent, on some level, feel anger. Remember, not all anger is bad, and neither is all conflict.

Conflict is an inevitable part of life, school, and relationships: miscommunication between a parent and a child; an argument between friends over money; aggravation when a driver cuts you off or somebody at church is mad at you and refuses to speak to you. At school, what if a classmate doesn't meet the deadline for his or her part of a combined project? How should you respond when an adult asks you to do something clearly unethical? Do you hold your tongue, wait to see what will happen, or confront, defend, maybe even blow up?
If you find yourself in one of these situations, do you hold back, or do you protest, fight, and insist on your rights?

Conflict can result in either problem-solving and resolution or all-out war! How we approach conflict greatly impacts the outcome. Having the right mind-set going into it won't guarantee peaceful resolution, but having a wrong mind-set will bring certain failure and continuing tension. As long we live on earth, we will experience conflict! And that's not always bad.

GOOD REASONS TO ACCEPT AND FACE CONFLICT

• To stand against wrong. For example, if someone is taking drugs or abusing alcohol – confronting them and challenging them to get help; holding your friend who stood you up accountable (or following through on consequences); going to court because you received a traffic ticket unfairly.

• To protect someone. For example, if a someone physically abuses a child.

• Because the situation, realistically and practically, just can't continue the way it is. For example, your relationship won't last much longer, or your teacher may fail you.

• Because of a clear sense of urgency or responsibility. For example, William Wilberforce's long but successful battle to end slavery in the British Empire in the nineteenth century.

• To seek and experience resolution and/or reconciliation. You're ready to make peace (to confess the ways you contributed to the conflict, forgive, negotiate), and you're pretty sure the other party is too.

• Because you know you need to make right your previous response or behavior during a conflict--to confess your faults, resolve the anger, ask forgiveness, etc.

THE IMPORTANCE OF COMPASSION WHEN FACING CONFLICT

What is compassion? It is the ability to enter into the mind and heart of another, to share his sorrow, to know him "from within," thus giving rise to mercy and understanding.

In the Revelations of Divine Love Julian of Norwich calls compassion a wound. It is so because human experience teaches us that if we love we suffer. It's therefore easier not to love, for if we do we give the other power to hurt us. The pains of those we love become our own, and the more we love the more we open ourselves to possible rejection, with its attendant emotions. If we love we "feel" for others, and the more we widen our hearts to include all, the more we shall find ourselves bearing the sorrows of the world. Elizabeth Ruth Obbard "Magnificat" pp 47, 49-50

A definition: Compassion means feeling what the other person feels, feeling with him or her, being able to put yourself in his or her shoes, caring enough to see his or her side.

The Holy Bible tells us to "Put on . . . compassion, kindness, humility, meekness, and patience, bearing with one another and, if one has a complaint against another, forgiving each other. . . . And above all these put on love, which binds everything together in perfect harmony." [1]

When facing conflict we face three crucial choices, and our answers make all the difference.

- Relationship or winning? If the latter, sooner or later you will lose the relationship. This is not a game!
- Connect or conquer? The first is servant-hood, the second pride.
- Love or dominate? Couples often quote the following at their weddings, "Love is patient and kind; love does not envy or boast; it is not arrogant or rude. It does not insist on its own way; it is not irritable or resentful." [2]

If a wrong, selfish attitude isn't put aside, the conflict will only increase.

Practical Strategies for Managing Conflict

Step 1: When you clash or disagree with another person, one way to prevent escalation is to take a break (time-out) to consider the issues and your response. Don't feel pressured to resolve the situation immediately. Withdraw from the person, not huffily or in condescension, but with kind words to the effect, "It's probably best if we talk about this later, when we've both cooled down and have had a chance to think over what's bothering us and what we really want to say."

But don't make the time-out open-ended; try to decide when you will get back together to talk (in ten minutes? tomorrow over dinner? Wednesday night after school?). Use the break/time-out to pray or meditate and determine what concerns you have or what requests you might make.

Step 2: Sum up what the other person says by paraphrasing his or her demands, viewpoints, and comments. Most people don't listen well and tend to react defensively when engaged in conflict. Summarizing what someone says doesn't mean agreement with the other person's opinion or request, but it does demonstrate that you are listening, that you care and are trying to understand.

- "In other words, you were not able to make your deadline, and you hope I can finish the project."

• "What I hear you saying is that you want me to make my friend pay 25 percent more than the normal cost."

Step 3: Communicate your need and viewpoint graciously but firmly.

• "I was able to complete my part of the project, but I do not have time to take on your portion as well."

• "I think that overcharging my friend is wrong and I can't ask him/her for more money than the normal cost."

Application: Write out a scenario in which you experienced conflict at school or at home. Envision how you could respond by using the time-out and sum-up skills and communicating your viewpoint.

Now do the same for a situation at home or in another setting.
Applying the sum-up skills and seeking wisdom will afford you greater opportunity for success in school or at home and in all your relationships.

Question: How can I control my anger when someone (a "downer") is unfairly blaming or judging me?

Answer: Here are some steps to take. First of all, listen attentively to what is being said. Try to understand and clarify the issue and don't defend yourself against character judgments, labeling, etc., until you've dealt with the issue and you both have cooled down.

Example:
Downer: "You didn't complete that project on time (or finish the room, house-cleaning, etc.)! You are just lazy and irresponsible!"

You: "You think I am irresponsible because I didn't finish the project. Is that right?"

Downer: "Yes! I could have finished the project myself along with everything else I am doing! You just don't care!"

You: "You think I don't care because I didn't finish the project; so you think you should have done it. I want to explain to you what happened. Are you willing to listen to me?"

Downer: "Yes. But I don't think you can give me any excuses for your irresponsibility."

You: "I didn't finish the project because some unexpected needs came up (or other responsibilities/assignments at school took precedence). I know that you are disappointed but I now have time to work on the project."

Downer: "OK. But, I'm still pretty angry about this."

You (now work toward resolution and confrontation about the character judgments): "I will do the project and have it done in a few days. But in the future, I am requesting that you refrain from making character judgments about me when you have a problem with my work."

Downer: "What do you mean by that?"

You: "I don't like being labeled irresponsible and lazy. When you need to approach me about some issue in the future, please keep to the issue--i.e. the behavior that bothers you and your feelings about it. This will help me feel respected and improve our relationship."

Foundational Insights:
Conflict is normal and a process which both parties, when willing, can work through. When conflict management skills along with compassion are applied to disputes – relationships can improve and successful resolution is possible.

Questions for Thought

1. What conflicts are you currently facing, or should you be facing, that it would be right for you to accept and handle?

How will you go about this?

2. Which of the Practical Strategies for Managing Conflict do you find the hardest? Why?

3. Have you been seeking to resolve some conflict but the other person is unwilling? Have you taken any of the steps from the model? What should be the next step, and when will you take it?

4. Take the empathy inventory. How can working on empathy skills--putting yourself in someone else's shoes--help you manage conflict more effectively?

5. What are the causes of conflicts? What can result from conflict?

6. Describe the reasons to accept and face conflict from this lesson:

7. What positive role can compassion play when you are facing conflict?

8. What does the quote: "I don't have to attend every argument I'm invited to" mean? Do you agree or disagree?

9. Summarize the steps in Practical Strategies for Managing Conflict. Write out a recent conflict you have experienced applying the steps to it. Use more paper.

10. What is your normal reaction when someone else unfairly accuses you of some wrong doing? Is the example in the book helpful? Why or why not?

11. How has your perspective on conflict changed? Are there any steps in conflict management you would like to apply from this lesson?

Project: **Interview some of your friends.**
Ask them:
What do you think of conflict?
What's your style?
Do you think conflict can be a good thing? Why or why not?
When have you experienced conflict resolution?
What helped bring about the resolution?

Share the interviews with your group or mentor.

12. **Scenarios:**

Barbara is 15 and a sophomore at a local high school. She has come for anger management due to a stressful relationship. About six months ago she was transferred from another high school. She has a locker next to Fred who condescending and critical. By the end of the day she often feels like she's "boiling." It is not uncommon for her to awaken in the middle of the night ruminating about an incident during the day.
She has tried to discuss it with Fred but he simply states, "I don't know what you're talking about and walks away." She then went to her Dean, but was told that she was being too sensitive. She reports feeling trapped in the situation.

    a. What are Barbara's triggers for being angry?

    b. In what ways can you identify with her?

    c. What skills would help Barbara manage her anger in a healthy way? Be specific.

Sam plays on a basketball team. During practice he has noticed that a team member – Allen – 'accidentally' trips, pushes or runs into him at least once a practice.
He is getting aggravated and wants to punch him out but has resisted.

    a. What are Sam's triggers for anger?

b. In what ways can you identify with him?

c. Which of the strategies for managing conflict would help Sam manage his anger in a healthy way and work through the conflict?

Assignment: Write out a conflict which recently caused you to become angry. Which skills did you or could you use to manage your anger?

Assignment: Write out a recent General Provocation Scenario from your own life. Keep a daily log of your anger. Complete the Anger Management Report weekly.

What are your Anger Survey results now from pg. 8? (circle one):

Category I   Category II   Category III

Please measure your use of anger coping skills from 1-10: _____
(1=poor use of skills   5=intermittent use of skills   10=consistent use of skills)

Lesson Eight: Turn Your Anger into Forgiveness

Goals: *To learn that forgiveness is possible and is a vital aspect of bringing the process of anger to a conclusion.*
To identify someone in your life with whom you need to ask forgiveness or forgive.

Resentment is like taking poison and waiting for the other person to die.

Malachy McCourt

To forgive is to set a prisoner free and discover that the prisoner was you.

Lewis B. Smedes

It's challenging to think about forgiving people who have hurt us, isn't it? We often don't want to let go of the painful memories of abuse, put-downs, broken promises and harsh words. I (Lynette) can remember when one of my sisters refused to give me my portion of our father's inheritance. I felt hurt and angry. It was difficult to forgive her, but in time I did with the help of God. The question is-- how can we unlock the door of forgiveness? First we need to understand some facts:
- Forgiveness, though difficult, is possible.
- Forgiveness is vital to resolving anger.
- Forgiveness is the road to personal healing and reconciliation with God and others.
- Forgiveness is an ongoing process.
- Forgiveness emulates the highest quality of humanity.
- Forgiveness sets you free from the past.

The Challenge of Forgiveness
Talking about forgiveness causes us to reflect on some very personal, hurtful experiences in our lives. We don't want to think about those times, and we find ourselves struggling to resolve the memories of pain and inflicted wounds by others.

What are some of the most challenging things to forgive?
People who are manipulative, abusive, irresponsible, who lie, cheat, are arrogant, disrespectful or inconsiderate? Forgiveness is a difficult topic because it calls us as human beings to a higher standard -- the standard of grace and mercy. But when we don't forgive we run into a greater human dilemma: that of unforgiveness -- where the pain of resentment and bitterness flows through our veins, quenching our spirits, breeding a cynicism about life, people, and God. Unforgiveness encases us in a miserable existence, changing our perception of the world and people from positive to negative, causing us to withdraw, priming us to see the world and people as hostile.

How would you define forgiveness? Here are some ideas:
- letting go of the blame.
- ceasing resentment.
- pardoning.

What forgiveness is and isn't
Forgiveness is a choice, not a feeling. Forgiveness is not fair, it is not easy, and it is hard work. Forgiveness is when you decide to let someone else off the hook--when you elect to not get paid back or take revenge for a wrongdoing. When you withhold punishment.
Forgiveness is not turning a blind eye or ignoring what happened.
Forgiveness is not forgetting or denying what happened.
Forgiveness is not the same as reconciliation.
Forgiveness doesn't justify, approve or excuse the offense or offender.
Forgiveness doesn't always remove the consequences of the offense from the offender.
Forgiveness is a process that may include confrontation and exhortation.

Why we need Forgiveness
The state of anger creates the need to forgive. As soon as we become angry at someone or something we need the sweet relief of forgiveness, not only to grant it to others but to receive it for ourselves. We need forgiveness to bring our lives back into a state of harmony and peace.

What do religious leaders and writers have to say about the importance and process of forgiveness?

Phillip Yancey wrote: *"Forgiveness is another way of admitting, 'I'm human, I make mistakes, I want to be granted that privilege and so I grant you that privilege'. Forgiveness breaks the cycle. It does not settle all questions of blame and justice and fairness: to the contrary, often it evades those questions. But it does allow relationships to start over. In that way, said Solzhenitsyn, we differ from all animals. It is not our capacity to think that makes us different, but our capacity to repent, and to forgive. Only humans can perform that most unnatural act; and by doing so only they can develop relationships that transcend the relentless law of nature."*
Josh McDowell wrote: *"Forgiveness is the oil of relationships."*

No matter what religious background you come from or belief you hold – it may help you to know that forgiveness is an important aspect of spiritual life. Christians are told to "forgive as Christ has forgiven you." [1] In Judaism, if a person causes harm, but then sincerely and honestly apologizes to the wronged individual and tries to rectify the wrong, the wronged individual is religiously required to grant forgiveness. Islam teaches that God is "The All-Forgiving." Forgiveness often requires the repentance of those being forgiven. In Buddhism, forgiveness is seen as a practice to prevent harmful thoughts from causing havoc on one's mental well-being.

Forgiveness cancels a debt someone owes us and restores the relationship when restoration is possible. It is the only solution in a world ridden with sin and evil to help us start over with people and discover peace.

Lynette writes: Months after not receiving my Dad's inheritance from one of my sisters –
I felt convicted to forgive her. I knew I had to let go of the anger. I wrote and told her how much I loved her and wanted to reconcile with her. It was not until thirteen years later that she and I finally reunited.

So how can you practically forgive someone who has hurt us? Here are some *Steps to Forgiveness*. Applying these steps to our lives can deliver us from bitterness and help us work toward forgiveness:

- Discover forgiveness: When you discover and experience forgiveness deeply in your own life, you have a foundation to offer forgiveness to those who have offended you. Many find their belief in God's forgiveness helps them forgive others also.
- Choose to forgive: You must make the decision to let go of bitterness and revenge and forgive others.
- Renew your mind: Challenge your mind with the truth and about how you need to be forgiven too. You may consider seeking your Higher Power for help in forgiving.
- Grant mercy: Empathize with those who have injured you. Recognize that forgiveness is the only way to be set free from the prison of resentment.
- Remember--forgiveness is a process: If you are stuck in unforgiveness, you can talk and pray with a confidante, a pastor, spiritual mentor, or a counselor to help you deal with the resentment and hurt you still feel. This will provide a context for release (of the painful feelings you are experiencing), support, and a better understanding of the person and situation.

When others hurt or abuse us, when they disrespect or humiliate us, we can forgive them. So don't think that your anger should be stuffed down, negated, or turned into bitterness. Your anger is an emotion and force that can be useful. You can decide to forgive because that is a mechanism for resolving the hurts and the unfairness of life.

Guidelines for Reconciliation and Forgiving

1. Deal constructively with the root cause of anger toward the offending party.
    a. Ask: What am I angry about? What is my responsibility?
    What is the other person's responsibility?
    b. Forego retribution.
    c. Pour out your anger in prayer or to a confidante.

2. Plan a constructive confrontation.
    a. Apologize, if appropriate. *This is an important step in taking responsibility for any way you have offended someone.*
    b. Use a soft, loving approach. Reflect on the fact that you need forgiveness as well.
    c. Be honest, yet tactful.
    d. Indicate the behavior change needed.

3. Choose to forgive.
    a. Release the other person from guilt and bondage.
    b. Let go of the demands you want to make on the other person.

4. Return good to the offending party.

5. Change your attitude toward the offending party.

Here is a question many people and writers ask:
Does Forgiveness = No Consequences? One thing I've been thinking about is: am I willing to treat a person who has hurt me as well as I would treat those I consider my closest friends (assuming that it's appropriate to interact with the person who hurt me)? It seems to me that until I am, I'm falling short of God's standards. Does it mean that there should be no consequences for the sin?

Answer: In his book, <u>Total Forgiveness</u> Kendall addresses the issue of how we treat others after they have let us down or mistreated us. There are consequences which sometimes can't be and shouldn't be removed when we forgive. He talks about how a woman forgave the criminal who raped her but, decided to testify in court in order to stop him from inflicting another crime. In that case, judicial consequences were meted out along with forgiveness.

Here are some of my thoughts: You may decide that a friendship may change because that person cannot keep confidences. A change in relationship is not the same as forgiveness. You can let go of the blame and let go of any punishment and continuing to hold the wrong against a person--but, you may learn something about that person's character: that they can no longer be trusted with confidences or that they are not empathic and tend to be harsh when you divulge a weakness about yourself or that they are not responsible in keeping their commitments.

Therefore, you may forgive them, but, will no longer:
  … become vulnerable and share your mistakes
  … share your problems with them, or rely on them to do a project with you, etc.

Forgiveness does not mean that you will:
  … trust all people on the same level or
  … expect all people to live up to certain standards or
  … relinquish the consequences for their wrongful behavior.

On the one hand, you can give someone another chance to start over but, on the other hand, there are times when you will need to set boundaries.
Forgiveness doesn't equal trust! Forgiveness doesn't mean there won't be consequences for the person. Forgiveness does not mean that boundaries will remain the same. Forgiveness will make you wiser. Forgiveness will challenge you at times to be vulnerable and to trust again. But, more importantly, forgiveness will set you free!

How to apologize if you have been rude, abrasive, curt, lied or shown negative anger toward someone else:
What can you do? First of all, take responsibility. Admit you were wrong and follow these simple steps by saying: "I'm sorry." "I was wrong." "Please forgive me."

It takes humility and self-awareness to confess your faults. In the long- run, you will grow as a person, become a better friend or family member and work towards reconciliation.

Foundational Insights:
Forgiveness sets you free from the prison of anger and resentment. Forgiveness ends the cycle of anger and blame moving you closer to reconciliation and new goals.

Questions for Thought

1. Can you think of examples of people who have totally forgiven those who offended them? Do these examples seem unrealistic, beyond your capability?
_____
_____

2. Which of the Steps to Forgiveness seems the most difficult for you? Why? What needs to happen to begin the process of forgiveness?
_____
_____
_____

3. Which of the Guidelines for Reconciliation and Forgiving did you find the most encouraging or helpful? Why?
_____
_____

4. Define forgiveness. What makes forgiveness an important part of anger resolution? What are the consequences of hanging onto resentment?
_____
_____
_____

5. Think of someone you can't forgive. List all the excuses you have for not forgiving:
   __ He/she has failed too many times.
   __ He/she will do it again.
   __ He/she will just take it for granted.
   __ He/she hasn't asked for forgiveness.
   __ The sin was too great.
   __ The pain is too much.
   __ I will not get over it.
   __ He/she deserves to be punished.
   __ He/she did it deliberately.
   __ He/she is not really sorry.
   __ other_____

6. Have you ever needed forgiveness? How does the quote by Phillip Yancey in this lesson affect your perspective on forgiveness?
_____

7. What will happen if you decide to forgive?

___

"Forgiveness is a choice not a feeling. Forgiveness is not *fair,* it is not easy, and it is hard work. Forgiveness is when you decide to *let someone else off the hook*--when you elect to *not get paid back or take revenge for a wrongdoing.* When you withhold punishment. Forgiveness *is not turning a blind eye or ignoring* what happened. Forgiveness is not *forgetting or denying* what happened. Forgiveness is not the same as *reconciliation.* Forgiveness doesn't *justify, approve or excuse* the offense or offender. Forgiveness doesn't always *remove the consequences* of the offense from the offender. Forgiveness is a process which may include confrontation and exhortation."

8. What is your opinion of this paragraph? How does this change your perspective on forgiveness?

___

9. What is the hardest aspect of forgiveness for you? Which Steps to Forgiveness are you willing to take? What will the consequences be in the long-run?

___

10. How might you go about asking someone you have offended for forgiveness?

___

11. Mary came home to find her brother wrecked her bedroom while she was at an after school activity. She blew up and demanded he clean it up. Her anger kept simmering and she found it hard to forgive even though he cleaned up the mess.

What's going on with Mary? Have you ever experienced this kind of anger?

___

How could she have handled the situation in a more appropriate manner?

___

12. What if Question:
What if your friend says something negative about your character behind your back?

Your anger quotient is: 1-10 (1=low; 5= moderate; 10=high) _____

Your response is:
_____
_____
_____

What's good about your response (thoughts, behavior)?
_____
_____

Describe the consequences of your response:
_____
_____

How does this help you achieve your goals?
_____
_____

What do you need to change? How could forgiveness play a part in your respond?
_____
_____
_____

The Prodigal Son Parable in "F"

Feeling footloose and frisky, a feather-brained fellow forced his fond father to fork over the family finances. He flew far to foreign fields and frittered his fortune feasting fabulously with faithless friends. Finally facing famine and fleeced by his fellows in folly, he found himself a feed-flinger in a filthy farmyard. Fairly famished he fain would have filled his frame with the foraged foods of the fodder fragments left by the filthy farmyard creatures. Fooey he said, My father's flunkies fare far fancier, the frazzled fugitive found feveringly, frankly facing facts.

Frustrated by failure and filled with foreboding he forthwith fled to his family. Falling at his father's feet, he floundered forlornly. Father, I have flunked and fruitlessly forfeited family favour. But the faithful father, forestalling further flinching frantically flagged the flunkies. Fetch forth the finest fatling and fix a feast. But the fugitive's fault-finding frater frowned on the fickle forgiveness of the former folderol. His fury flashed.

But fussing was futile, for the far-sighted father figured, such filial fidelity is fine, but what forbids fervent festivity? The fugitive is found! "Unfurl the flags, with fanfares flaring! Let fun

and frolic freely flow!" "Former failure is forgotten, folly is forsaken! And forgiveness forms the foundation for future fortitude."
Author unknown

> Assignment: Write out a recent General Provocation Scenario from your own life. Keep a daily log of your anger. Complete the Anger Management Report weekly.
>
> What are your Anger Survey results now from pg. 8? (circle one):
>
> Category 1   Category 11   Category 111
>
> Please measure your use of anger coping skills from 1-10: _____
> (1=poor use of skills; 5=intermittent use of skills; 10=consistent use of skills)

Lesson Nine: When to Take a Break

Goals: *To explore how to apply taking a break for managing anger. To implement this coping skill to help de-escalate anger.*

When angry count to ten before you speak. If very angry, an hundred.

Thomas Jefferson

Speak when you are angry and you will make the best speech you will ever regret.

Dr. Lawrence J. Peter

You may ask, "How do I know when to take a break? Usually I am well into the fight or argument before I know what is happening, and I can't stop the escalation. I feel like I have no control."

Step 1 is recognition of what makes you easily frustrated. What are your triggers? Against which people and in what situations does your anger escalate? Go to the provocation scenario to find out. Maybe you already know you are easily frustrated by:
- someone's tone of voice,
- the use of certain demeaning or critical words,
- glaring looks,
- disregarding or disrespectful behavior,
- someone not listening to you,
- feeling overwhelmed or helpless.

Step 2 is to be ready to say you have to take a break from such situations as soon as they occur. Anger rears its ugly head in less than a second! That does not give you much time to prepare, analyze, and control yourself.

Now that you have determined the times, situations, and people that trigger your anger, follow these guidelines:

- Take a deep breath. (This will help your body calm down some and will help clear your mind.)
Pray. (Many people have found this helpful.)
- Tell the other person: "I have decided to take a break to consider the issue(s) or problem(s)." It's good to have a prepared statement since anger can keep you from thinking clearly. (Write it out in your own words on a card and keep it in your pocket or purse if that helps.) "I will get back to you by _____." (Give a reasonable time-frame.)
- Don't apologize for taking a break. Nehemiah did this, and so can you!
- Move to another part of the house, do something to cool down, listen to soothing music, do relaxation exercises, take the dog for a walk.

When you are in your break period:
- Evaluate the scenario between you and the other person.
- Decide what the issue is and what your concerns are.
- Determine what you want or need. What request can you make?
- How can you reconcile if this is necessary or possible?
- Review Handling Anger Effectively, the assertiveness and conflict lessons and apply the recommended steps to your situation.
- Determine if you are struggling with any cognitive distortions and challenge your thinking with reality and the truth.

Foundational Insights:
Taking a break is essential to stop the escalation of (physiological) anger and conflict, calm down, identify the issue as well as your perspective and thoughts, and plan an intelligent approach for managing the conflict.

Questions for Thought

1. How often does anger escalate beyond control in your life? How have you tried to avoid or control this? Would taking a break help? Why or why not?
___
___
___

2. What triggers generally make your anger skyrocket?
___
___
___

3. Why do you find it so hard to take a break? How do you feel (or how do you think you would feel) when you announce you need to take time to think things over?
___
___
___

4. What effect has taking a break in the past had on your anger?
___
___
___

5. When have you applied the break or time-out to cool off? How did it help?
___
___
___

6. What are the suggested steps involved in a taking a Break (Time-out) from the book? Write these out on a 3x5 card and/or your Smart phone, Iphone, Ipad, computer, tablet, nook, kindle as a reminder.

7. List the situations when you need to take a time-out or a break:

8. Reflect on this principle from the Good Book: *"take note of this: Everyone should be quick to listen, slow to speak and slow to become angry, for man's anger does not bring about the righteous life that God desires."* (NIV) [1]   Is this at all helpful to you? How?

9. **What if Question:**
What if one your parents promises you can go on a vacation with your friend and then they start hedging on the decision? Both of you begin to raise your voices.

Your anger quotient is: 1-10 (1=low; 5= moderate; 10=high) _____

Your response is:

What's good about your response (thoughts, behavior)?

Describe the consequences of your response:

How does this help you achieve your goals?

What do you need to change? How could taking a break or time-out help the situation?

Assignment: Write out a recent General Provocation Scenario from your own life. Keep a daily log of your anger. Complete the Anger Management Report weekly.

What are your Anger Survey results now from pg. 8? (circle one):

Category 1   Category 11   Category 111

Please measure your use of anger coping skills from 1-10: _____
(1=poor use of skills; 5=intermittent use of skills; 10=consistent use of skills)

Lesson Ten: *Plan to Change Your Life by Changing Your Thinking.*

Goals: Determine how thinking can escalate angry feelings and behavior. Investigate how to change thinking that is distorted and unrealistic.

Anger blows out the lamp of the mind.

Robert Green Ingersoll

It is important to recognize how much thinking impacts your feelings and can trigger your anger. Circle which type of thinking is true of you. If you cannot evaluate your type of thinking, ask a confidante or close friend or family member to give you feed-back.

Use the anger log sheet to evaluate examples of your thinking during angry scenarios. Compare and contrast it with this list to see where you might be struggling with cognitive distortions.

1. *All-or-nothing thinking*: You see things in black-and-white categories. If your performance is less than perfect, you consider yourself a total failure.
Give an example of how you may think this way. For example: "I always come-up short."
"I am just a failure." "I can't handle this."
Do you feel like a total failure at times? Example: "I can never make it work."

Is this a distortion of the truth?

Do others tell you that you are not seeing things clearly?

How often does this thinking pattern occur?
    daily   weekly   more than once a day   several times a day

With whom?   Where?

2. *Over-generalization*: You see one negative event as an unending pattern of defeat. Example: "We are always fighting" (even though this only happens once a week).

When do you think this way? What do you tell yourself?

How often does this thinking pattern occur?
    daily   weekly   more than once a day   several times a day

With whom?   Where?

3. *Mental filter*: One negative detail or event is all you can dwell on. Thus you think that most of life is pretty negative as well. Do you always see the cup as half-empty? Example: "We would have had a great time at the picnic, but the mosquitoes almost ate us up!"
Do you dwell on the negative?

How often does this thinking pattern occur?
    daily   weekly   more than once a day   several times a day

With whom?   Where?

4. *Disqualifying the positive*: You believe that positive experiences "don't count" for some reason or other. So you maintain a negative belief about your life even though circumstances contradict it.
Describe when this type of thinking occurs: Example: "Even though I got a good evaluation, I know my teacher hates me."

How often does this thinking pattern occur?
    daily   weekly   more than once a day   several times a day

With whom?   Where?

5. *Jumping to conclusions*: You automatically make a negative interpretation even though there are no definite facts that really support your conclusions.

How and when does this kind of thinking occur?

Example: "My friend showed up late; he/she must not like me."

How often does this thinking pattern occur?
    daily   weekly   more than once a day   several times a day

With whom?   Where?

a. *Mind-reading*: You indiscriminately conclude that someone is reacting negatively to you, and you don't bother to check it out. Example: "He/she went to lunch with another friend, so he/she must be mad at me."

When and how does this happen?   What do you tell yourself?

How often does this thinking pattern occur?
    daily   weekly   more than once a day   several times a day

With whom?   Where?

b. *The fortune-teller error*: You anticipate that things will turn out badly, and you feel convinced that your prediction is an already-established fact. Example: "I know I'm going to fail this class" (even though you are getting good grades).

When and how does this happen? What do you tell yourself?

How often does this thinking pattern occur?
    daily   weekly   more than once a day   several times a day

With whom?   Where?

6. *Magnification (catastrophizing) or minimization*: You exaggerate the importance of things (such as your goof-up or someone else's achievement), or you inappropriately shrink things until they appear tiny (your own desirable qualities or the other person's imperfections). This is also called the "binocular trick."
When and how does this happen? What do you tell yourself? Example: "He always wins" (even though you won the chess game last week) or "my body is too fat" (even though you have been told you are the right weight).

How often does this thinking pattern occur?
    daily   weekly   more than once a day   several times a day

With whom?   Where?

7. *Emotional reasoning*: You assume that your negative emotions necessarily reflect the way things really are: "I feel it; therefore it must be true."

When and how does this happen? What do you tell yourself?

If you fall into this category, you are depending on your feelings as the measure of truth.

How often does this thinking pattern occur?
    daily   weekly   more than once a day   several times a day

With whom?   Where?

8. *"Should" statements*: You try to motivate yourself with "shoulds" and "shouldn'ts", as if you have to be whipped and punished before you can be expected to do anything. "Musts" and "oughts" are also offenders. The emotional consequence is guilt. When you direct should statements toward others, you feel anger, frustration, and resentment. Example: "I should clean the house in two hours." This is also a sign of perfectionism.

When and how does this happen? What do you tell yourself?

How often does this thinking pattern occur?
    daily   weekly   more than once a day   several times a day

With whom?   Where?

9. *Labeling and mislabeling*: This is an extreme form of over-generalization. Instead of describing your error, you attach a negative label to yourself. Example: "I'm a loser." When someone else's behavior rubs you the wrong way, you attach a negative label to him or her: "She/he's a loser." Mislabeling involves describing an event with language that is highly colored and emotionally loaded.

When and how does this happen? What do you tell yourself?

How often does this thinking pattern occur?
    daily   weekly   more than once a day   several times a day

With whom?   Where?

10. *Personalization*: You see yourself as the cause of some negative external event that in fact you were not primarily responsible for.
When and how does this happen? Example: "If I had prayed more, my son wouldn't have had a car accident."

What do you tell yourself?

How often does this thinking pattern occur?
    daily   weekly   more than once a day   several times a day

With whom?   Where?

This material has been adapted from Resource for Cognitive Distortions (revised) by D. Burns.

Foundational Insights:
Distorted and irrational thinking and expectations tend to escalate anger and conflict.
When distorted thinking is challenged with reality and truth--effective anger management is possible.

Questions for Thought

1. What three cognitive distortions did you most identify with?
_____
_____
_____
_____
_____
_____

How does it or they affect your life (be as specific as you can)?
_____
_____
_____

2. How does this kind of thinking contribute to your anger? How does this thinking distort your view of yourself, your parents and/or your friends?
_____
_____
_____

3. Do you tend to magnify situations or minimize? Do you use a mental filter or jump to conclusions? Do you tend to personalize or mind-read? Are you a fortune-teller or do you label others?
_____
_____
_____

4. Ask yourself: What if I were to give the other person the benefit of the doubt rather than judging him/her harshly? What would happen if I let go of the distorted thinking and believed the best about someone with whom I disagree or who disappoints me?
_____
_____

Try Humor Instead of Anger

Next time you are really livid about an inconvenience--like poor service--try making your point with humor instead of anger:
David went with his family to a fancy restaurant. Everyone ordered clam chowder. David noticed a gritty texture in the soup, scowled, and began to complain angrily. His nine-year-old son, Matt, also noted the grit but replied with a grin, "The clams are so fresh, you can still taste the sand in them!"

Log Your Thinking

An angry man is again angry with himself when he returns to reason.

Publilius Syrus

We encourage you to make a log of your thinking patterns as you use this course. Making a transition from unhealthy to healthy thinking is at times a difficult process but an important one.

Here is an example of faulty thinking:
"My friend showed up late for our dinner together. I concluded he/she really didn't want to be with me" (mind-reading).
What is the truth about this situation or person?

Describe the facts of the situation:
"Mary/Hank had a flat tire on the way to my house, which kept her/him from arriving on time. Therefore I should question the conclusion that she/he doesn't want to be with me. Maybe my low self-esteem is causing me to mind-read and jump to this negative conclusion."

We need to challenge such faulty thinking.

1. Give an example of a time when you used faulty thinking such as a time when someone overlooked your needs or preferences.
_____
_____
_____

What is the truth about this situation or person?
_____
_____
_____

Describe the facts of the situation:
_____
_____
_____

Ways to challenge my faulty thinking:
_____
_____
_____

2. Give another example of a time when you used faulty thinking.
_____
_____

What is the truth about this situation or person?
_____
_____
_____

Describe the facts of the situation:
_____
_____
_____

Ways to challenge my faulty thinking:
_____
_____

3. What faulty thinking similarities do you see in the situations you have logged?
_____
_____
_____

4. What will it take for you to believe the facts and truth versus your faulty thinking when you are confronted with anger-provoking situations?
_____
_____
_____

What's Good About Anger? Expanded Book & Workbook for Teens

PLAN TO CHANGE YOUR LIFE BY CHANGING YOUR THINKING

As you make such a plan and put it into action, the following questions and steps will be helpful:

1. What pattern of cognitive distortions do you see in your own Thinking? Which distortions occur most often?

_____
_____
_____

2. How can you challenge your thinking and bring about change?

_____
_____
_____

3. This quote provides a challenge and a goal to aspire to: *"Finally, whatever is true, whatever is honorable, whatever is just, whatever is pure, whatever is lovely, whatever is commendable, if there is any excellence, if there is anything worthy of praise, think about these things."* [1]

What effect will thinking the best of others versus the worst have on you? Is it possible?

_____
_____

4. How has your negative thinking pattern affected you emotionally, mentally, and spiritually- maybe even physically?

_____
_____
_____

5. What can you do to begin changing your faulty thinking?

_____
_____
_____

Examples:
- Make a log of your faulty thinking patterns, and challenge them with the truth. ___
- Read inspirational resources daily, pray often. ___
- Talk with a confidante, counselor, pastor, and advisor. ___

6. How can you begin to think about whatever is true, noble, right, pure, lovely, admirable, and excellent?

_____
_____
_____

How will thinking like this affect your life?

_____

Will you be less depressed? Less anxious? More optimistic? More hopeful?

7. Do you really want to get better? What would your life be like if you were more hopeful and optimistic?

_____

8. Have you tried such a plan before? Did it work? Why or why not?

_____

9. Which of these steps do you think will be the hardest? Why? What would help make it easier?

_____

10. How do you feel about the question, "Do you really want to get better?" Be honest. Why do you think this question is either fair or unfair? Helpful or irritating?

_____

11. What will it take for you to believe the facts and truth versus your faulty thinking when you are confronted with anger-provoking situations? How can you start believing the best about others (parents, teachers, friends, employers) who may irritate you?

_____

12. Describe how thinking patterns and distortions can have anger-provoking effects?

_____

> Assignment: Write out a recent General Provocation Scenario from your own life. Keep a daily log of your anger. Complete the Anger Management Report weekly.
>
> What are your Anger Survey results now from pg. 8? (circle one):
>
> Category 1   Category 11   Category 111
>
> Please measure your use of anger coping skills from 1-10: _____
> (1=poor use of skills; 5=intermittent use of skills; 10=consistent use of skills)

Look back on all the progress reports. What skills have you applied?

What is your anger quotient now?

Lesson Eleven: How Emotional Intelligence Impacts Anger

> **Goal:** To learn the importance of emotional intelligence - identifying how to empathize with others.

The ability to understand and regulate emotions as well as understand the emotions of others and handle relationships constructively = emotional intelligence.

Emotional Intelligence Skills Help You Manage Anger

What does emotional intelligence have to do with managing anger? Maybe you are wondering, "Why should I learn about emotional intelligence? If I am keeping my anger in check, that should be enough."

Experts have discovered that people with a high degree of emotional intelligence (EI) are more motivated to manage their anger, get better results, and build healthy relationships. Wouldn't you like to experience the kind of life where anger no longer dominates you, but becomes one of the tools you use to achieve your goals and experience a more satisfying life?

Let's first take a look at the meaning of EI. Daniel Goleman writes, "Emotional intelligence is the ability to recognize your own feelings and those of others, motivate yourself, manage your emotions well and in your relationships."

Growing in anger management skills is helpful. But developing EI will improve your life in greater ways. How? Ari Novak, Ph.D., LMFT, a leader in Anger Management, attests to the importance of EI in managing anger. He states, "After treating clients with anger-related issues for over 7 years, I have come to realize that increasing skills in Emotional Intelligence (EI) is one of the most effective interventions a person can learn. EI skills improve performance in so many areas of life including leadership, intimate relationships, and simple day to day situations."

How Emotional Intelligence Works

When you develop Emotional Intelligence you become adept at the following:

1. *Self-awareness.* Self-awareness is having the ability to identify your own emotions, strengths, and weaknesses. This foundational step in EI provides the ability to monitor your feelings and determine what triggers your anger. People who lack self-awareness of feelings are more prone to becoming ensnared by them and being left at their mercy. By gaining the skills to watch carefully and oversee your feelings, particularly your anger, you will be able to identify what the issues are and make better decisions about responding to difficult situations. Find out how you are doing in the area of self-awareness by reviewing the "Anger Survey," "Power of Anger," and "Managing Stress" lessons.

2. ***Self-management.*** Self-management is the ability to effectively be in control of your motives and regulate your behavior. Self-management is built on self-awareness and provides the capacity for bouncing back from failure or disappointments. By gaining the ability to apply the cognitive and behavioral skills found in this book, you will become more proficient at controlling unhealthy anger and emotions and building effective skills to guide anger into assertiveness, problem-solving, forgiveness, time-outs, and healthy self-talk. Examine the lessons covering these skills and determine your level of progress in applying them.

3. ***Self-motivation.*** Self-motivation is monitoring and controlling one's emotions in order to achieve goals. This ability delays immediate and temporary gratification by stifling impulsiveness in order to accomplish projects and long-term objectives. When you see the bigger picture of reaping the consequences for your actions, you will be self-motivated to redirect your anger and emotions into healthy communication and behavioral skills. The concept of this book is that "you can have good anger." That idea has motivated many people to change. Go back to the "When Anger is Good" lesson. Ask yourself, "What consequences have I experienced from unhealthy anger? What are the pros for expressing my anger in healthy ways? How does this motivate me to change?"

4. ***Social awareness.*** Social awareness is gaining empathy for other people. Empathy is the capacity to understand what others are saying and feeling and why they feel and act as they do. Empathy is built on self-awareness, self-management, and self-motivation. When you are able to empathize, you will put yourself in other people's shoes, understand their feelings and viewpoints, and consider their needs. Review the "Managing Conflict" lesson. How have you applied the Sum-Up skill? What has been the result? Read the rest of this lesson to really learn the importance of and how to apply empathy.

5. ***Relationship development.*** Relationship development is the capacity to act in such a way that you are able to influence others without controlling them. This allows you to achieve personal and relational goals. When you employ assertiveness and empathy skills and negotiate issues while considering the best interests of all parties, you will develop healthy and compatible relationships with others. Your relationships will improve when you cultivate assertiveness, empathy, and conflict management skills.

Dr. Pfeiffer, writes, "The development of Emotional Intelligence initially means to recognize-- actually feel--the sensations of frustration, annoyance, and anger in your body. Maybe you feel these in the form of tension in your chest, or you notice your face getting warm or red, maybe your hands are beginning to sweat. Once you are familiar and aware of these bodily sensations you are now ready to begin talking about your emotions as you actually experience them. The process of recognizing, experiencing and talking about your emotions puts you on the road to understanding and having compassion for yourself and then the ability to understand that others also have emotions too . . . you now have the capacity for empathy."

The Next Step: Learning to Empathize With Others
In order to really develop EI, we encourage you to focus on how to be a more empathic person as this is the key to social awareness and is critical to relationship compatibility.

First, take the empathy inventory found at the end of this lesson. Afterward come back and finish reading this lesson in order to identify the importance of developing empathy.

What is empathy?
Empathy is authentically listening to and understanding someone else's point of view. It's about seeing the situation from the other person's perspective. Empathy requires the ability to identify feelings and care about other people enough to consider their opinions and views, even when theirs differ from your own. Empathy will help decrease your frustration and anger-triggers because you will be focused on thinking about the other person's needs and not just your own.

Why is empathy important?
Empathy is the key to social awareness and is thus a key for defusing anger. By exploring someone else's viewpoint and feelings and putting yourself in the other person's shoes, you will be more likely to give the other person the benefit of the doubt and less likely to hold on to anger and resentment.

Gaining skills of listening to others and empathizing with them are essential for building relationships, defusing conflict and anger, and truly connecting with other people. It can build your relationships with those you interact with at your school such as friends, teachers, and if you work -- with coworkers. It can also help bond, bridge, and mend personal relationships with family members, and friends.

Most of us spend 70% of the day communicating. With nearly three-quarters of our day spent communicating, you would think that listening would compose half of that communication. Yet only 45% of our time communicating with others is actually spent listening.

Listening and empathy skills are foundational to interpersonal communication, and yet surprisingly we are rarely taught these skills in the classroom or from our parents.

It is insulting to be ignored, interrupted, or neglected. We all want to be heard and understood. We want others to really care and understand our feelings and opinions. We want to know we matter. We want validation. And yet we have difficulty giving to others the very thing we want from them.

How is empathy expressed?
One of the best ways to validate and connect with others is to ask them questions about themselves and to really listen to their response. This "active listening" is briefly discussed in the lesson on Managing Conflict.

People love to talk about themselves. Write out some questions in advance of meeting with people that you can ask to help you find out more about who they are and what their lives are like. Then be prepared to genuinely listen. After they have shared, paraphrase what they have said. If you can paraphrase and summarize what someone has said to you, you will send the message that you were listening, you understand and care for that person. Listening and paraphrasing is one of the most effective and important ways to validate someone. Taking the time to understand someone and enter into their world is the first step to becoming an empathetic person. Empathy goes the extra mile. It listens with the heart. We all know what it means to really listen. Listening is more than hearing and processing words. Listening understands, affirms, and accepts the other person's meaning, experience, and feelings.

Here are some benefits from practicing good listening and empathy skills:
• You are able to care for and understand the other person. Often the conversation is directed toward emotional issues that are very important to others. As a result, people will enjoy talking to you and will open up more.
• Even if you misunderstand others, you allow them to correct your interpretations. As a consequence, you are able to grow and learn more about other people.
• You let the speaker know that you, the listener, accept the speaker. In return the other person will feel more comfortable telling his or her story and feelings to you. Since the speaker feels safe to talk about personal subjects with you, he or she will be more vulnerable by expressing his or her deeper emotions, exploring his or her emotions and problem-solving.
• It decreases any frustration or anger you may have.
• It can also promote forgiveness because we gain a greater understanding of the other person's experience.
• It can prevent or reduce negative assumptions about others because empathy helps us build understanding of the other person.
• It fosters meaningful, helpful, and close friendships.

You may be thinking that this is too much. You have enough problems and concerns of your own. You don't have the time or desire to concern yourself with other people and their needs. Or maybe you feel angry that no one has shown empathy to you and so you do not wish to show empathy to others. Perhaps you just want to "live your life" and not be bothered with learning and practicing empathy skills. But there's something in it for you, too. When you are empathetic with others, they are more likely to show empathy toward you. And as you practice empathy, you too will benefit from your actions as you will be on your way to liberating yourself from the negative patterns of bitterness and anger.

We believe that when you build your emotional intelligence skills, you will discover a greater ability to manage your anger, get better results, and experience healthy relationships. Challenge yourself to really grow by writing out and applying the following questions and assignments. Then you will discover the kind of life where anger no longer controls you but becomes one of the tools you use to achieve your goals and experience a more fulfilling life.

Foundational Insights:
Developing empathy is key to promoting deeper connection and understanding between people. Empathy provides awareness and sensitivity for the other person's point of view and experiences – thus defusing anger, cognitive distortions and conflict.

The following inventory is designed for personal use and for discussion. Check the characteristics and tendencies which best describe you thoughtfully and honestly. Do not score or read the instructions on the next page until you have completed the inventory. Permission is granted to provide one copy of the inventory and examples to the facilitator or group leader for feedback. Complete any examples required as instructed on the scoring page.

Empathy Inventory: © copyright 2016 by Lynette J. Hoy, NCC, LCPC

1. When I am talking with someone – I find it hard to listen: ___
2. When someone is speaking I generally am thinking about I want to say and miss what they have said: ___
3. When someone is speaking I usually ask clarifying questions so I can understand what they have said:___ (check if you go back later with clarifying questions)
4. When others are talking I try to paraphrase or summarize what they said: ___
5. When someone is talking about a problem I try to pick up on their feelings and say, "you seem stressed out by school (or work) or disappointed with your life": ___
6. Others have told me I am a good listener: ___
7. People come to me when they have problems for encouragement: ___
8. I try to see things from other people's point of view even when I disagree with them: :___
9. I try to impress on others the point I want to get across: ___
10. I turn conversations around or change the topic so I can say what I believe is really important: ___
11. I have difficulty identifying feelings and emotions in myself: ___
12. I have difficulty identifying feelings and emotions in others: ___
13. When someone seems troubled I generally ask them what is happening: ___ Provide a recent example here:
14. When someone doesn't share my opinion I either explain myself in greater detail or stop talking to the person:___
15. I can easily identify strengths and weaknesses in my life: ___
16. When someone shares a problem and their feelings – I explore what may be the cause with them: ___
17. When my goals are in contrast to others – I usually try to negotiate with those in disagreement: ___
18. Most people say that I am a caring, thoughtful person: ___
19. People complain that I am "self-centered": ___
20. Significant people in my life say that I am driven to achieve my goals: ___
21. Some people say that I'm a poor listener: ____
22. People say that I am able to manage my anger and emotions: ___
23. I don't find it necessary to pressure people into believing the way I do about something important to me: ___
24. I try to imagine what it's like to be in someone else's situation and what they might be experiencing: ____
25. When someone is angry or frustrated with me I have a hard time listening to their complaint or remarks: ___

Score the Empathy inventory:
A. Numbers 1, 2, 9, 10, 11, 12, 14, 19, 20, 21, 25 = 0 (zero).
B. Add 1 point each for numbers: 3, 4, 5, 6, 7, 8, 13, 15, 16, 17, 18, 22, 23, 24.
(provide recent examples for each one of the B category statements on another sheet)

Empathy rating: 0= Heartless; 2-4= Low; 5= Half-hearted; 6-10= Moderate; 11-13= High; 14= Bleeding Heart.

Questions for Thought

1. Write out 2-3 sentences that describe your understanding of emotional intelligence.
_____
_____

2. How can developing EI help you achieve your goals in your life and in your relationships? How might developing EI impact your home or school situation?
_____
_____

3. What is your opinion on the importance of empathy? How can empathy have an impact on your anger?
_____
_____

4. Circle your final score on the empathy inventory: Empathy rating: poor = 1-4; moderate = 5-10; high = 11-14.

5. From the Empathy Inventory provide recent examples of the "B" statements you checked on a separate sheet.
_____
_____
_____
_____

6. On a scale from 1-10 (1 being the lowest and 10 the highest) how motivated are you to develop empathy skills? Share your reasons for being motivated or unmotivated.
_____
_____
_____
_____

7. How will supportive, empathic communication change your relationships?
_____
_____

8. Write out and practice the paraphrasing skills found in the "Assertiveness" lesson this week.
_____
_____

9. In order to determine your growth in self-awareness, self-management, and self-motivation, complete the following questions:

    a. From the survey in lesson one which kind of people and situations generally trigger your frustration and anger?

    b. How do you normally try to calm yourself down? What phrases or thoughts help defuse your anger?

    c. What skills from the book do you regularly apply to stressful situations that trigger anger or frustration?

    Assertiveness:___
    Empathy:___
    Break or Time-Out:___
    Problem-Solving:___
    Changing Self-Talk or Cognitive Distortions:___
    Forgiveness:___
    Stress Management and Relaxation:___
    Prayer:___

    d. What motivates you to develop EI?

    Rate your motivation level here:
    Low (1-3):___ Moderate (4-6):___ High (7-10):___

10. In order to determine your growth in social awareness, empathy, and constructive relationships, complete the following questions:

    a. Take the empathy inventory again in the appendix and rate yourself:___

    b. What skills are you applying to manage conflict and work through relationship misunderstandings?

        Paraphrasing, Sum-Up:___
        Active listening:___
        Time-out:___
        Assertiveness:___

Problem-solving:___
Forgiveness:___
Other:___

c. What steps will you take this week to grow in empathy skills with your friends/parents?

d. Which skills from the conflict lesson will help you develop healthier relationships?

e. How will forgiveness play a part in enhancing your relationships?

11. What is your understanding of emotional intelligence? How can developing EI help you achieve your goals in life and relationships?
_____
_____
_____
_____

12. How might developing EI impact your family life or school relationships?
_____
_____

13. What is your opinion of the importance of empathy? How can empathy affect your anger?
_____
_____
_____

14. How did you score on the empathy inventory?
Empathy rating: poor = 1-4   moderate = 5-10   high = 11-14

What steps will you take this week to grow in empathy skills?
_____
_____
_____

15. From the Empathy Inventory - provide recent examples of the 'B' statements you checked on a separate sheet.
_____
_____
_____
_____

16. **What if Question:**
What if you are ruminating about how your parent mistreated you or a friend disrespected you?

Your anger quotient is: 1-10 (1=low; 5= moderate; 10=high) _____

Your response is:
_____
_____
_____

What's good about your response (thoughts, behavior)?
_____
_____

Describe the consequences of your response:
_____
_____

How does this help you achieve your goals?
_____
_____

What do you need to change? How could empathy help your response/attitude?
_____
_____

17. Complete all questions and share your answers with your group, therapist, coach or mentor.

18. Compare and contrast your previous anger management progress reports with this week's report.

Assignment: Write out a recent General Provocation Scenario from your own life. Keep a daily log of your anger. Complete the Anger Management Report weekly.

What are your Anger Survey results now from pg. 8? (circle one):

Category 1   Category 11   Category 111

Please measure your use of anger coping skills from 1-10: _____
(1=poor use of skills; 5=intermittent use of skills; 10=consistent use of skills)

Lesson Twelve: Building Healthy & Successful Relationships

Goal: Identify ways to build healthy relationships through empathy skills and supportive communication and thus, defuse conflict and anger.

Great relationships connect deeply resulting in closeness, collaboration and intimacy!

Validation and assertiveness are keys to helping you connect deeply with people. The *first key in connecting* is to be able to validate others through active listening and what is called "entering someone else's world"...One of the best ways to communicate you respect is to ask them questions about themselves and to really listen to what they say to you and pick up on their viewpoints through paraphrasing. You don't have to agree with their opinions, but you can show you value him or her as a person by *really* listening.

People love to talk about themselves- so be prepared to ask them some questions which will help you find out more about who they are and what their life is like. Then be prepared to really listen and paraphrase what they say. If you can paraphrase and summarize what someone has said to you, you will send the message that you understand and care for him/her. This is one of the most important ways you can validate another person.

When a friend says to another friend -
"Of course, what you have to say is important, it just isn't very interesting"-- his judgmental remark will cause her to feel invalidated, hurt and angry. *Asking questions and communicating support through paraphrasing skills expresses your value for someone else. Again,* you may not agree with what they are telling you, but, you can express understanding about what their life is like.... their problems, their struggles... This also helps you begin to empathize with people because you start putting yourself in their place and enter their world.

Validation is also expressed by communicating support and paraphrasing what someone is saying. When supportiveness and paraphrasing skills are combined with assertiveness the results are remarkably effective. With practice anyone can learn it!

SUPPORTIVENESS SKILLS:
These are abilities that help build trust and understanding between you and someone else and which communicates, "I'm on your side."

OPEN RESPONSES: This is the ability to communicate openness to help facilitate gaining further information, even if that information may be critical or emotional.
"....Say more about . . ."
"....I'm confused about . . ."
"....Spell that out further . . ."
"....Give me a specific example so I can understand more clearly."

Practice the following:
Open Responses:
-One person says, "You obviously don't care very much about older people!" You respond:
_____
_____

-Someone says, "I always thought that you cared about community values. I can see now I was wrong." You respond:
_____
_____

-You've heard from others that the neighbor next door is upset with you. You go to the neighbor and say:
_____
_____

(Use one of these open responses to explore further what the person next to you said about his/her motivation to attend the group or the goals he/she began considering because of the last session.)

UNDERSTANDING RESPONSES are best accomplished by paraphrasing: This is the ability to demonstrate to someone else, especially an antagonist, that you understand what he or she is trying to communicate. Paraphrasing is stating in your own words what the other person said.
First- Focus on the speaker (You . .)
Second- Be brief
Third- Summarize the Fact/Feeling

Here are some ways to help you paraphrase (repeated here from the assertiveness section):
  "In other words..."
  "Let me get this straight..."
  "So you felt that..."
  "What I hear you saying is..."
  "If I understand you correctly..."
  "Would you say that ...?"
  "Do I understand you to mean...?"   "Do you mean...?"

Paraphrasing: Here are some Specific examples of Paraphrasing for empathic responses:
  "You were really scared"
  "You'd rather stay home because you are stressed out"
  "You feel frustrated"
  "You felt it was very unfair for me to . . ."
  "From your perspective I was not being helpful when I . . ."
  "You were inspired to change when your teacher gave you a better grade or praised you…."

If you can enter into another person's world by reflecting back and paraphrasing what they have said--you will demonstrate empathy, concern and earn their respect. You will build bridges which draw you closer.

Let's try practicing these skills….
~~Ask your friend: Describe a stressful event that recently occurred.
Paraphrase what the person says.
_____
_____

Ask him/her: *How did you feel when I paraphrased what you said?*

Understanding Responses:
How would you paraphrase this complaint? Practice:
Your parent says, "I just don't know how I'm going to make ends meet. We've had extra doctor bills this month. Then the car transmission went out & had to be replaced. Now you say you want to drive. How are I am going to afford the insurance?"

You say:
_____
_____

Understanding responses....
Paraphrase the following:
Your friend or lab partner says, "I'm trying my best to do a decent job. But how can I get everything done when there is so much to do?"

You say:
_____
_____

These skills will help you connect with people by validating what they say through paraphrasing skills. You don't have to agree with what the person says. But you can show them you *respect* them and that you are interested in them and *heard* what they said through these skills.

It is also important to be prepared to talk about yourself and to *develop the art of assertiveness as taught in previous lessons. Assertiveness is the second key to connecting with people.*

Foundational Insights:
Everyone wants to be understood and respected. Everyone wants to be heard. We can demonstrate our concern and respect for others by through active listening and supportiveness skills. We can defuse conflict and anger through empathy.

Questions for Thought

1. What are some personal characteristics for building great relationships? How will supportive, empathic communication change a relationship?
_____
_____
_____

2. How do you respond when someone really listens to you and displays empathy? Think of an example of when someone expressed empathy towards you.
_____
_____

3. Describe how the supportiveness skills can change anger and conflict escalation?
_____
_____
_____

4. Apply some of these skills to a recent provoking scenario which escalated into conflict. How would the scenario have turned out if you had applied the supportive and/or paraphrasing skills?
_____
_____
_____

5. Write out the understanding and paraphrasing responses on a 3x5 card to memorize.
_____
_____

Assignment: Write out a recent General Provocation Scenario from your own life. Keep a daily log of your anger. Complete the Anger Management Report weekly.

What are your Anger Survey results now from pg. 8? (circle one):

Category 1   Category 11   Category 111

Please measure your use of anger coping skills from 1-10: _____
(1=poor use of skills; 5=intermittent use of skills; 10=consistent use of skills)

Lesson Thirteen: Choosing Behavior Alternatives

Goals: *To learn the impact of thinking on behavior and feelings and challenge negative thinking. To apply healthy skills for defusing anger.*

It is important to recognize how much your thinking impacts your feelings and can trigger your anger.

Have you ever wondered what makes you do the things you do? Some people say, "I felt like doing it – so I did!" What underlies your behavior? Is it feelings or thinking and choices? Is it someone's behavior?

If you are an *"all or nothing" thinker* – you may make some hasty, regrettable decisions and not consider other options since your thinking is too limited. If you are a person who *"catastrophizes or exaggerates"* events, you may avoid taking action and making a decision or you may lash out aggressively because you fear losing control. Either way distorted thinking will escalate your feelings of frustration and anger and not get you what you want - better relationships, satisfaction, healthy goals.

If you are a *"mind-reader,"* you most likely will misjudge someone's intentions and falsely accuse them, strike out at them or withdraw from the relationship. Unfortunately, mind-readers usually make poor behavior choices based on their thinking versus the reality of the situation. No one can judge another person's motives. Only God can.

What about when your thinking is on-target and not distorted? You have looked at the event or the situation or person -- tried to be objective and given the benefit of the doubt to the person. Maybe you have asked God for His perspective on it. If this is the case, then, you are ready to make some choices about the action or next step you can take.

Thinking → Choices → Actions → Feelings and Consequences

The above formula demonstrates the impact of thinking on behavior. What you think and believe is the basis for your choices and actions. Consequences for those actions will follow.

New Options and Choices for Behavior/Actions
Write out what usually happens when you get angry:

When I was angry about _____ I decided to _____ and the following resulted: _____ (I hurt someone or the other person is not speaking to me now).

When I was angry about _____ I decided to _____ and the following resulted: _____ (I got in trouble with the law).

When I was angry about _____ I decided to _____ and the following resulted: _____ (I got drunk or broke something, etc.).

Complete the following questions to make a behavior change plan:

1. What were the problems or issues which angered you?
_____
_____
_____

2. What did you need?
_____
_____
_____

3. How could you have behaved differently and changed the situation and consequences?
_____
_____
_____

4. What could you have communicated by using some of the assertive suggestions in the book?
_____
_____
_____

5. How will the changes you want to make help you achieve healthy goals and relationships?
_____
_____
_____

6. According to questions 3, 4 and 5 – what can you do differently this week to handle issues or situations which frustrate you?
_____
_____

I will_____(ask my sibling kindly to wash the dishes or take out the garbage) by _____(date).
I will_____(re-do an assignment to get a better grade or consult with a pastor or counselor, etc.) by _____(date).

7. Write out three situations in which you would like more self-control. Apply the steps from the Handling Anger Effectively lesson and some assertiveness skills. Use a separate sheet if necessary.

_____
_____
_____

8. What happens when you begin to get angry? Write out what the triggers are and how you usually respond:

_____
_____
_____
_____

9. What other type of response or behavior can you choose for the above scenario?

_____
_____

10. Describe times when you have been angry and responded differently – in a healthy versus destructive way:

_____
_____
_____

Foundational Insights:
It's easy to just lash out when you are angry or say something unkind. Anger is a strong emotion but, it is how you think and perceive events which cause the emotion to rear its ugly head. Often thinking is incorrect or extreme because of underlying fears or unfounded judgments and perceptions. Correcting and challenging thoughts and perceptions will impact your behavior and feelings.

Assignment: Write out a recent General Provocation Scenario from your own life. Keep a daily log of your anger. Complete the Anger Management Report weekly.

What are your Anger Survey results now from pg. 8? (circle one):

Category I   Category II   Category III

Please measure your use of anger coping skills from 1-10: _____
(1=poor use of skills; 5=intermittent use of skills; 10=consistent use of skills)

Lesson Fourteen: Defusing Anger & Hostility. Dealing with Bullying

Goal: Clarify origins of and learn to defuse anger & hostility. Identify steps to handle bullying.

Hostility, bullying and harmful anger are unacceptable attitudes and behaviors
Lynette J. Hoy

Anger, hostility and bullying are not the same. These attitudes and associated behaviors may be combined but, have very different characteristics. We have defined anger as an emotion or energy which can be good and healthy when turned into faith, assertiveness, conflict resolution, empathy, problem-solving and forgiveness. On the other hand, anger is harmful when people become aggressive, violent or emotionally and verbally abusive. Here are some definitions:

Anger- A negatively toned emotion, subjectively experienced as an aroused state of antagonism toward someone or something perceived to be the source of an aversive event.

Hostility- An attitudinal disposition of antagonism toward another person or social system. It represents a predisposition to respond with aggression under conditions of perceived threat.

Part One: Defusing Anger and Hostility
What can you do when you are confronted with an angry or hostile person? Here are some steps:

Begin To Defuse Early
Angry and frustrated people usually indicate their mood prior to opening their mouths and beginning a hostile attack. One way to address or pre-empt the attack is to begin the defusing process before the other person gets on an abusive rant. For example, if you notice someone is agitated or frustrated -- say, "This must be difficult for you. Can you share what's going on?"

LISTEN to the aggrieved party and allow a short time of "airing" of the grievance without comment or judgment. Some people call this the 'magic minute'. Listening to someone, especially to someone who is not happy, for a full minute can be difficult! The temptation to interject a comment or ask a question will be overwhelming; it must be resisted.

NOTE: The only exceptions to this would be if they are use obscenities, threatening or profane language or if they are being offensive. Every person's concerns should be heard, but you have the right to be treated civilly and not be subjected to abusive language, threats or harassment. Should this happen, it is appropriate to draw the line and say, "I really want to listen to your concern, but I can't do so if you continue to use foul (threatening) language."

Allowing the person to vent (appropriately versus rudely or threateningly) for 30 seconds or a minute and then, responding with support: "I can see you are stressed out and that you have concerns."

When they begin to cool down: "I would like to discuss your concerns further and work towards some solutions. Can I ask you some questions?" *It's important to identify if the person is calming down and sincerely wants to talk this over with you or if you are at risk of harm. Remember you have the right to end the conversation if it escalates or you feel you are in danger.

If You Lose Control, You Lose, Period!
Manipulative nasty behavior is designed to affect you emotionally so that you will become aggressive or defensive. When you lose our cool and defend ourselves or become aggressive you actually end up doing what the other nasty person wants us to do…and you lose because you enter into an ugly game where nobody can win. Self-control is critical, and that has a particular meaning. It means that you control your behavior. You are entitled to be angry or upset if you choose but you can learn to control your behavior and the way you express that anger or upset so something good comes from it. Here are some tips:

• When dealing with someone who is attempting to provoke a confrontation, make a conscious attempt to slow down your responses. Do NOT reply immediately since your first gut level response is likely to be an angry or defensive response. Before you respond, ask yourself the questions: "How can I deal with this situation so I create LESS anger and upset on both sides?" Then respond.

• Pay special attention to the speed and loudness of your speech. When people get excited they tend to talk more quickly and loudly and that causes the other person to escalate also…as the conversation increases in speed there is less and less thought and more chance that people will say things that are destructive. Take your time.

• If you are really triggered, ("ticked off") at what is being said to you, it is a good idea to take a time-out. A time-out is not avoidance--it differs in terms of what one says. For example, if you say: "I'm not talking about this with you" that is an avoidance response and a brush-off and likely to make the situation worse. If you say: "It isn't a good time for me to talk about this, but I would like to discuss it with you tomorrow. Can we set up a time to meet?" That's different because it is expressing a commitment to work with the person and does so without characterizing the conversation as negative.

In the case of a bully or very hostile person – you may not be able to discuss the problem or issues rationally. In those cases – it's best to stay away from that person or report him/her to authorities if you feel at risk of harm.

Be Assertive, Not Manipulative, Passive or Aggressive
You have a right to take action, or impose consequences in situations where someone has stepped over the line in their comments or behaviors. In fact, if you don't speak up in these situations bully-type people will perceive you as an acceptable victim for their poor behavior. When using assertive type statements or setting up consequences, do not dwell on the way the person is communicating any more than necessary. Make your statement, and then refocus the conversation back to the issue.

Example:
"Peter, I want to work through this with you. In order to do that I need you to slow down, and clarify some questions so we can get this done."

Notice that the above is firm, clear and assertive. If Peter persists in being nasty or personal it is within your rights to say:

"Peter, if you can answer my questions -- I can get all the facts and try to work through this with you. If you continue to raise your voice I'm going to have to end this conversation and leave. Which would you prefer?"

Use the Broken Record Technique
The Critical Message: "It Isn't Going To Work With Me"
Aggressive, abusive and manipulative people look for victims they can control, using a variety of confrontation-provoking behavior. When dealing with such people the important message to send is "What you are doing isn't going to work with me. . ."
Scenarios:

1. Bob regularly harasses you about the ways you dress or speak and points it out in front of others. He calls you names like 'slut', 'stutterer' or 'ugly'.

How have you responded to these kinds of situations? What could you do differently? How does understanding the other person help you not take their anger and hostility personally? What strategies might work well for you?

Part Two: Preventing & Interrupting Bullying

What is Bullying? When someone is habitually overbearing, harsh or cruel, typically using manipulation, intimidation or harassment to overwhelm, dominate or control you and others.
This is a person who is perpetually angry and hostile.

Bullying is unwanted, aggressive behavior among youth that involves a real or perceived power imbalance. The behavior is repeated, or has the potential to be repeated, over time. Both kids who are bullied and who bully others may have serious, lasting problems.

In order to be considered bullying, the behavior must be aggressive and include:
An Imbalance of Power: Kids who bully use their power—such as physical strength, access to embarrassing information, or popularity—to control or harm others. Power imbalances can change over time and in different situations, even if they involve the same people.
Repetition: Bullying behaviors happen more than once or have the potential to happen more than once.
Bullying includes actions such as making threats, spreading rumors, attacking someone physically or verbally, and excluding someone from a group on purpose.

There are three types of bullying:
Verbal bullying is saying or writing mean things. Verbal bullying includes:
Teasing
Name-calling
Inappropriate sexual comments
Taunting
Threatening to cause harm

Social bullying, sometimes referred to as relational bullying, involves hurting someone's reputation or relationships. Social bullying includes:
- Leaving someone out on purpose
- Telling other children not to be friends with someone
- Spreading rumors about someone
- Embarrassing someone in public

Physical bullying involves hurting a person's body or possessions. Physical bullying includes:
- Hitting/kicking/pinching
- Spitting
- Tripping/pushing
- Taking or breaking someone's things
- Making mean or rude hand gestures

Where and When Bullying Happens

Bullying can occur during or after school hours. While most reported bullying happens in the school building, a significant percentage also happens in places like on the playground or the bus. It can also happen travelling to or from school, in the youth's neighborhood, or on the Internet.

Frequency of Bullying

There are two sources of federally collected data on youth bullying:

The 2009 Youth Risk Behavior Surveillance System (Centers for Disease Control and Prevention) indicates that, nationwide, 20% of students in grades 9–12 experienced bullying.

The 2008–2009 School Crime Supplement (National Center for Education Statistics and Bureau of Justice Statistics) indicates that, nationwide, 28% of students in grades 6–12 experienced bullying.

What's your typical response when someone is angry or hostile towards you?

a. Get angry too ___
b. Walk away ___
c. Tell them off ___
d. Tune-out ___
e. Write them off ___
f. Think "not another hot-head!" or "I can't take this!" ___
g. Try to understand and listen to their problem ___
h. Give up "they're all alike" ___
i. Put yourself in their shoes ___
j. Let them know by your expression how irritating they are ___
k. Let them know in no uncertain terms that their behavior is inappropriate ___
l. Feel defensive ___
m. Wish they would just go away. ___
n. Think "let's get this case over" ___
o. Believe 'they deserve it'. ___

What are the consequences of these attitudes & responses? Escalation of anger? De-escalation of anger? How will people feel or respond if you tune them out, are short with them or have a negative attitude towards them? It's hard to respond effectively or appropriately to an angry or hostile person. Consider the following.

Principle: How you respond to a bully or hostile, angry person -- is a sign of your ability to control yourself. If you get defensive, angry or irritated -- you give them control over your response. When you control your response – you may have the ability to de-escalate a hostile situation. On the other hand, there may be no negotiating or talking over issues with a bully.
So, you need to diagnose the situation and decide if the 'bully' is dangerous. Recognize that talking with or responding to a real bully may tend to escalate his/her anger and hostility. In that case – protect yourself. Leave. Call 911 or someone in authority.

Be Aware of Classic bullying characteristics:

1. Recurring outbursts
2. Serious threats
3. Intentional harassment
4. Harsh ridicule

Bullying cover-ups: A bully's favorite statements when confronted about his/her ridicule are:

"I was just kidding."
"Why are you so sensitive?"
"You need to lighten up."
"You need to learn to take a joke."
"What's the matter, can't you take a little ribbing?"

So, how can you keep calm when confronted by a bully or an angry/hostile person? Anger is like a disease! It's contagious!
Remember: "You don't have to attend every argument you're invited to."

First, remember not to take it personally then, apply the Thinking Ahead reminders recommended previously:
- Keep your breathing even
- Take it one step at a time
- What helps you calm yourself down?

Review the lesson on Conflict Management. Practice the sum-up and communicate viewpoint skills. If the person is not a true 'bully' but, is having a bad day or is angry – you may be able to talk the situation over without escalation.

Bullying and Violence Prevention

The following information is included to raise the awareness of these special teen issues. Anger Management programming can play an important part in preventing teen bullying and violence.

The National Youth Violence Prevention Resource Center writes:

Bullying among children and teenagers has often been dismissed as a normal part of growing up. Little attention has been paid to the devastating effects of bullying, or to the connection between bullying and other forms of violence. In recent years, however, students and adults around the country have begun to make a commitment to stop bullying in their schools and communities.

What is bullying?

Bullying includes a wide variety of behaviors, but all involve a person or a group repeatedly trying to harm someone who is weaker or more vulnerable. It can involve direct attacks (such as hitting, threatening or intimidating, maliciously teasing and taunting, name-calling, making sexual remarks, and stealing or damaging belongings) or more subtle, indirect attacks (such as spreading rumors or encouraging others to reject or exclude someone).

How common is bullying?

Almost 30 percent of teens in the United States (or over 5.7 million) are estimated to be involved in bullying as either a bully, a target of bullying, or both. In a recent national survey of students in grades 6 to 10, 13 percent reported bullying others, 11 percent reported being the target of bullies, and another 6 percent said they bullied others and were bullied themselves. Limited available data suggest that bullying is much more common among younger teens than older teens. As teens grow older, they are less likely to bully others and to be the targets of bullies.

Bullying occurs more frequently among boys than girls. Teenage boys are much more likely to bully others and to be the targets of bullies. While both boys and girls say others bully them by making fun of the way they look or talk, boys are more likely to report being hit, slapped, or pushed. Teenage girls are more often the targets of rumors and sexual comments. While teenage boys target both boys and girls, teenage girls most often bully other girls, using more subtle and indirect forms of aggression than boys. For example, instead of physically harming others, they are more likely to spread gossip or encourage others to reject or exclude another girl.

How does bullying affect teens that are the targets of bullies?

Bullying can lead teenagers to feel tense, anxious, and afraid. It can affect their concentration in school, and can lead them to avoid school in some cases. If bullying continues for some time, it can begin to affect teens' self-esteem and feelings of self-worth. It also can increase their social isolation, leading them to become withdrawn and depressed, anxious and insecure. In extreme cases, bullying can be devastating for teens, with long-term consequences. Some teens feel compelled to take drastic measures, such as carrying weapons for protection or seeking violent revenge. Others, in desperation, even consider suicide. Researchers have found that years later, long after the bullying has stopped, adults who were bullied as teens have higher levels of depression and poorer self-esteem than other adults.

Bullying can also affect those teens who witness the bullying.

In one study of junior high and high school students, over 88 percent said they had witnessed bullying in their schools. Teens who witness bullying can feel guilty or helpless for not standing up to a bully on behalf of a classmate or friend, or for not reporting the incident to someone who could help. They may experience even greater guilt if they are drawn into bullying by pressure from their peers. Some teens deal with these feelings of guilt by blaming the victim and deciding that he or she deserved the abuse. Teens sometimes also feel compelled to end a friendship or avoid being seen with the bullied teen to avoid losing status or being targeted themselves.

Which teens are most likely to become bullies?

While many people believe bullies act tough in order to hide feelings of insecurity and self-loathing, in fact, bullies tend to be confident, with high self-esteem. They are generally physically aggressive, with pro-violence attitudes, and are typically hot-tempered, easily angered, and impulsive, with a low tolerance for frustration. Bullies have a strong need to dominate others and usually have little empathy for their targets. Male bullies are often physically bigger and stronger than their peers. Bullies tend to get in trouble more often, and to dislike and do more poorly in school than teens who do not bully others. They are also more likely to fight, drink, and smoke than their peers.

Teens who come from homes where parents provide little emotional support for their children, fail to monitor their activities, or have little involvement in their lives, are at greater risk for engaging in bullying behavior. Parents' discipline styles are also related to bullying behavior: an extremely permissive or excessively harsh approach to discipline can increase the risk of teenage bullying.

Surprisingly, bullies appear to have little difficulty in making friends. Their friends typically share their pro-violence attitudes and problem behaviors (such as drinking and smoking) and may be involved in bullying as well. These friends are often followers who do not initiate bullying, but participate in it.

As mentioned above, some teenagers not only bully others but are also the targets of bullies themselves. Like other bullies, they tend to do poorly in school and engage in a number of problem behaviors. They also tend to be socially isolated, with few friends and poor relationships with their classmates.

What are the long-term consequences of bullying behavior?

Bullying is often a warning sign that children and teens are heading for trouble and are at risk for serious violence. Teens (particularly boys) who bully are more likely to engage in other antisocial/delinquent behavior (e.g., vandalism, shoplifting, truancy, and drug use) into adulthood. They are four times more likely than nonbullies to be convicted of crimes by age 24, with 60 percent of bullies having at least one criminal conviction.

What can schools do to stop bullying?

Effective programs have been developed to reduce bullying in schools. Research has found that bullying is most likely to occur in schools where there is a lack of adult supervision during breaks, where teachers and students are indifferent to or accept bullying behavior, and where rules against bullying are not consistently enforced.

While approaches that simply crack down on individual bullies are seldom effective, when there is a school-wide commitment to end bullying, it can be reduced by up to 50 percent. One effective approach focuses on changing school and classroom climates by: raising awareness about bullying, increasing teacher and parent involvement and supervision, forming clear rules and strong social norms against bullying, and providing support and protection for all students. This approach involves teachers, principals, students, and everyone associated with the school, including janitors, cafeteria workers, and crossing guards. Adults become aware of the extent of bullying at the school, and they involve themselves in changing the situation, rather than looking the other way. Students pledge not to bully other students, to help students who are bullied, and to make a point to include students who are left out.

If You Are Being Bullied...

Talk to your parents or an adult you can trust, such as a teacher, school counselor, or principal. Many teens who are targets of bullies do not talk to adults because they feel embarrassed, ashamed, or fearful, and they believe they should be able to handle the problem on their own. Others believe that involving adults will only make the situation worse. While in some cases it is possible to end bullying without adult intervention, in other more extreme cases, it is necessary to involve school officials and even law enforcement. Talk to a trusted adult who can help you develop a plan to end the bullying and provide you with the support you need. If the first adult you approach is not receptive, find another adult who will support and help you.

It's not useful to blame yourself for a bully's actions. Remember, the bully is the one with the inappropriate behavior. The bully treats people with cruel intentions and has a behavior disorder. You can do a few things, however, that may help if a bully begins to harass you. Do not retaliate against a bully or let the bully see how much he or she has upset you. If bullies know they are getting to you, they are likely to torment you more. If at all possible, stay calm and respond evenly and firmly or else say nothing and walk away. Sometimes you can make a joke, laugh at yourself, and use humor to defuse a situation.

Strategies for preventing and handling bullying:

1. Act confident. Hold your head up, stand up straight, make eye contact, and walk confidently. A bully will be less likely to single you out if your project self-confidence.

2. Try to make friends with other students. A bully is more likely to leave you alone if you are with your friends. This is especially true if you and your friends stick up for each other.

3. Avoid situations where bullying can happen. If at all possible, avoid being alone with bullies. If bullying occurs on the way to or from school, you may want to take a different route, leave at a different time, or find others to walk to and from school with. If bullying occurs at school, avoid areas that are isolated or unsupervised by adults, and stick with friends as much as possible.

4. If necessary, take steps to rebuild your self-confidence. Bullying can affect your self-confidence and belief in yourself. Finding activities you enjoy and are good at can help to restore your self-esteem. Take time to explore new interests and develop new talents and skills. Bullying can also leave you feeling rejected, isolated, and alone. It is important to try to make new friendships with people who share your interests. Consider participating in extra-curricular activities or joining a group outside of school, such as an after-school program, church youth group, sports team or a martial arts program.

5. Do not resort to violence or carry a gun or other weapon. Carrying a gun will not make you safer. Guns often escalate conflicts and increase the chances you will be seriously harmed. You also run the risk that the gun may be turned on you or an innocent person will be hurt. And you may do something in a moment of fear or anger you will regret for the rest of your life. Finally, it is illegal for a teen to carry a handgun; it can lead to criminal charges and arrest.

If Someone Else is Being Bullied…

1. Refuse to join in if you see someone being bullied. It can be hard to resist if a bully tries to get you to taunt or torment someone, and you may fear the bully will turn on you if you do not participate, but try to stand firm.

2. Attempt to defuse bullying situations when you see them starting up. For example, try to draw attention away from the targeted person, or take the bully aside and ask him/her to "cool it." Do not place yourself at risk, however.

3. If you can do so without risk to your own safety, get a teacher, parent, or other responsible adult to come help immediately.

4. Speak up and/or offer support to bullied teens when you witness bullying. For example, help them up if they have been tripped or knocked down. If you feel you cannot do this at the time, privately support those being hurt with words of kindness or condolence later.

5. Encourage the bullied teen to talk with parents or a trusted adult. Offer to go with the person if it would help. Tell an adult yourself if the teen is unwilling to report the bullying. If necessary for your safety, do this anonymously.

Question

What are the causes and consequences of violence and bullying? How can you prevent violence and bullying?

_____
_____
_____
_____
_____
_____

Preventing Bullying:

1. Avoid the Bully

Avoiding the bullies will prevent them from having physical interaction with you. You cannot skip school altogether, but find different routes to take to class to limit the interaction with the bully.

2. Always Stay With a Friend.

Find friends that will walk with you around school and that will stand by you if you are bullied. Bullies tend to pick on loners who appear weak, because bullies are weak themselves. They thrive on making others feel bad because they have inadequacies themselves. There is safety in numbers, so always walk in a crowd.

3. Don't Be Afraid to Stand up for Yourself!

It is okay to say no and to talk back to a bully. If you stand up for yourself, there will be less chance of the bullying continuing. Do it at the first instance, and don't let the feelings fester.

4. Do Not Wear Your Heart on Your Sleeve

Hide your feelings. A bully just wants to get a reaction out of you. Tears or screaming is the perfect reward for a bully. Whatever you do, do not show your feelings. A bully just wants to see you hurt.

5. Tell a Friend or Teacher

Do not cover up for a bully. Tell someone -- a friend, teacher or parent. If someone knows what is going on, then they can be there to protect you. This also creates a verbal "paper trail" and a case against the bully should there be legal action against the person bullying you.

6. Do Not Bully Back

Do not fall into the cycle of bullying back. When kids are bullied, sometimes they tend to do the same to others because they are frustrated. Bullied kids can act out towards parents, siblings and friends because they know they can use their voice against them. Bullies take power away and their victims often want to get their power back -- sometimes at the expense of others.

Do Not Blame Yourself

You are not the problem, the bully is. The bully is the one with the need to make you feel bad, and you did not do anything to cause the bully to come after you. A bully wants to break you down, and if he cannot succeed, he will stop or move on.

Find a Safe Place

If you cannot always be in a group, find a safe place to hang out when you are not in class. Go to a teacher's classroom, the main office or a place you will be safe.

Protect Yourself and Be Prepared

You can fight back if you are physically attacked first. In some states, such as Washington, you must be hit twice before you can justify self-defense. Know the laws in your state, and if you are physically attacked, do not be afraid to defend yourself. Take martial arts classes so that you can learn how to protect yourself.

Find Ways to Make New Friends

If you do not have support at your school, get involved in other places such as a church group, volunteer organization or other place where you will be surrounded by positive people. Positive people give you energy to deal with bullies who want to ruin your day. If you are positive and unbreakable, the bully will leave you alone.

How to Deal with a Bully at School

Learning how to deal with a bully at school presents some real challenges for the victim of bullying. While bully victims desperately want to stop the bully, many are afraid to ask for help. Feelings of shame and embarrassment, or a fear of appearing weak, often keep kids from admitting to an adult that there is a problem. This can actually make the bullying worse; the bully suffers no consequences for his actions, and may actually feed on the continued power and control he has over his victim.

Victims Need Help

When bullying continues for long periods of time, the victim can suffer serious effects, such as anxiety, depression, poor academic performance and poor self-image. Some bullying victims even suffer physical illnesses, such as headaches and stomach aches, as a reaction to their fear and anxiety of dealing with the bully. In the most extreme cases, kids have been driven to suicide or acts of lethal violence against others. It's essential for kids who are bullied to find relief from the problem before it becomes severe.

Tell Someone

If you are the victim of bullying, the most important thing to remember when trying to decide how to deal with the bully is that you must tell an adult whom you trust: a parent, a teacher, a school counselor or anyone else you can count on. There is no need to be embarrassed about being bullied. You are not at fault. No one deserves to be verbally, psychologically or physically assaulted, ever. If you feel you are being bullied, tell someone immediately, before the situation gets out of control.

Prevent Bullying

There are other things you can do to prevent yourself from becoming a victim. One of the biggest reasons why people bully is because it gives them a feeling of power. Bullies enjoy feeling as though they can be in control of other people. Ignoring a bully can be surprisingly effective. If you walk on by, with your head held high, you send the message that you are not giving him that power; you will not allow yourself to be controlled.

Bullies often prey on people that they perceive as being weak or lacking in confidence, so by walking tall and projecting an image of confidence and strength, you will show them that you are not a willing victim. While you may not always feel strong, it's important to remind yourself of your own strengths often. Everyone is good at something, and by focusing on your assets, you can be proud of yourself and your accomplishments. That pride will certainly show in how you carry yourself.

Questions

1. What have you learned about bullying?
   _____
   _____
   _____

2. Do you fit the description of a bully? Describe. Take the Controller/Abuser survey on page 43. What was your score?___
   _____
   _____

3. What characteristics of controllers/abusers are similar to bullies?
   _____
   _____
   _____

4. What steps can you take to stop bullying behavior?

   ___Identify if you have bullying characteristics (take the controller/abuser survey)

   ___Begin to identify your triggers for anger (grow in self-awareness)

       What are your triggers?

   ___Implement strategies which help interrupt unhealthy anger; bullying and aggression (refer to lesson material such as time-out; stress management; changing self-talk)___

       Which skills have you tried?

   ___Learn to communicate your needs and resolve conflict in a healthy way (assertiveness and empathy skills)

5. What motivates you to stop bullying? Think about how bullying has harmed your goals and relationships:
   _____
   _____
   _____

6. If you or someone you know is being bullied – what helpful steps will you take from this lesson?
   _____
   _____

Lesson Fifteen: Accepting Responsibility for Unhealthy Anger

Goal: Acknowledge and take responsibility for harmful anger. Identify the consequences for your actions.

When you take responsibility for your behavior and anger – you begin to control it.

It's not easy to own-up to our faults or lack of responsibility. When you are late to school – you tell the teacher the traffic was horrible or your parent didn't wake you up.

When you fail to work part-time to pay for extra clothes or activities – you accuse your parents for not caring enough to increase your allowance.

Blaming defined is: making it look like someone else is responsible for your misbehavior.

Why is it so difficult to own-up? Why do people keep blaming and shirking responsibility or accepting consequences for their behavior? Maybe it has to do with pride? Maybe you learned that it worked to keep blaming and made *you* look good and *someone else* look bad. Maybe it's hard to be humble. Maybe it has to do with needing to be in control again.

Whatever the reason or excuse you make for blaming and not accepting responsibility – *it is not in your best interest or in the interest of building character and relationships* to continue on this path.

How does blaming and not taking responsibility contribute to anger? It creates within you a defensive reaction. When situations occur and you are confronted with the truth of your behavior or you suffer consequences – you tend to blame it on someone else such as your parents, teachers co-workers or friends. You displace your anger onto someone else because you don't want to own-up. You don't want to feel bad about yourself or look bad in front of others. Blaming keeps you from being honest and taking the responsibility. You may feel better temporarily – but, in your heart you know the truth. You know you need to own-up.

The first step is to admit you have been living this way. Write out the situations when you have blamed someone or something else for your irresponsible behavior.

Make a Plan to Change:

Describe the situation:
_____
_____
_____

How did you react to the consequences?
Did you blame someone else or minimize your behavior?
___
___
___

How has this kind of behavior (blaming/irresponsibility) affected your life or relationships?
___
___

How did it affect your anger quotient? Re-take the anger survey in the book and evaluate your response.
___
___
___

Replay the scenario in your head. Who was really to blame? Maybe you were only partially at fault…
___
___
___

How could you have responded by demonstrating responsibility?
___
___
___

What would have happened if you took responsibility? How would this have affected the conflict, your anger quotient and your relationship(s)?
___
___
___
___

Foundational Insights:
Taking responsibility is not easy. Taking responsibility means that you have to identify your on-going strengths and weaknesses. It means you have to be willing to become vulnerable. It may mean that you incur a negative consequence at work, in the community or at home.

Positive, long-lasting results generally come from taking responsibility vs. shifting the blame to someone else. People will trust you and your word. People will accept apologies from you. People may be more apt to own-up to mishaps and more apt to apologize to you. You will no longer have to hide behind a banner of blaming.

Questions for Thought

1. Is irresponsibility unhealthy? Sinful? Greedy? Can it result in rage, slander and lying?
_____
_____
_____

2. How will taking responsibility promote integrity in your life?
_____
_____
_____

3. How will it affect your anger? Describe:
_____
_____
_____

4. How will your relationships be affected if you take responsibility and own-up to your mistakes, failures and poor attitudes?
_____
_____
_____

5. How will your spiritual life change if you take more responsibility for your actions?
_____
_____
_____

6. **What if Question:**
What if your sibling doesn't clean up his/her mess & you can't use the family room?

Your anger quotient is: 1-10 (1=low   5= moderate   10=high) _____

Your response is:
_____
_____

What's your real response? "_____ is so lazy and never takes responsibility."   yes   no

What's good about your response (thoughts, behavior)?
_____
_____

Describe the consequences of your response:
_____
_____

How does this help you achieve your goals?
_____
_____

What do you need to change? How could applying one of the skills help the situation?
_____
_____

7. Explore the cognitive distortion(s) that you struggle with which contribute to blaming and irresponsibility:
_____
_____
_____

8. What specific change could you make this week to foster healthier relationships with others by taking more responsibility?
_____
_____
_____

9. Review the assertiveness lesson. How can assertiveness (not aggressiveness) help you take responsibility?
_____
_____
_____

Assignment: Write out a recent General Provocation Scenario from your own life. Keep a daily log of your anger. Complete the Anger Management Report weekly.

What are your Anger Survey results now from pg. 8? (circle one):

Category 1   Category 11   Category 111

Please measure your use of anger coping skills from 1-10: _____
(1=poor use of skills; 5=intermittent use of skills; 10=consistent use of skills)

Lesson Sixteen: Facing the Consequences of & Interrupting Aggression

Goal: Clarify origins of and learn alternatives to aggressive behavior.

Consequences can be motivators for positive change

One of the major reasons you are taking this course is due to consequences you have incurred because of acting out your anger. Maybe you got in trouble with the law. Maybe you were involved in a "road rage" incident. Maybe your behavior became threatening or violent or you injured someone else or someone's property. Maybe drinking triggered an angry outburst. In any case, you are suffering the consequences of expressing your anger in a harmful way.

Your anger has disrupted your life. It may have caused a rift between you and a significant person in your life. Your anger may have caused you to lose your reputation. In the long-run – suffering these consequences can motivate you to gain greater control over your anger. Experiencing the consequences may help you to rebuild your life and relationships.

Personally, you may be struggling with a lot of regret over your actions as well. Feelings of guilt and shame and remorse may overcome you at times. You may have lost sleep, experienced changes in your appetite or kept ruminating over the events. Learning to deal with these emotions is a consequence as well.

You may still blame the other person who you think incited you to anger. You may be dealing with a growing resentment and urge to get revenge. Working through these thoughts and emotions is necessary. You will need to clarify what your responsibility was and is and what the other person's responsibility was and is. You may never be reconciled – if this person was a stranger as in the case of road rage. It's up to you to choose the road of forgiveness versus the road of "getting even."

The most important question you can ask yourself is: "How can I allow the consequences I have incurred to change me for the better?" What *can* you get out of this?

When you commit to changing your behavior and managing anger you can experience the following:
1. Personal growth and control over my emotions.
2. Improved relational skills and healthier relationships.
3. Greater sense of dignity.
4. Reconciliation with God and others.
5. No fear over further consequences with the law or fear of failing a class, losing money, relationships, etc.
6. More satisfying life.
7. No shame or guilt because of angry outbursts.

The following points if applied to your life will interrupt unhealthy responses to anger such as aggression or outbursts. Consider how you can apply these to situations you regularly encounter.

Keys to Stopping Aggression or Lashing out:

1. *Taking a Break (Time-out)*:
Taking a break from the situation is one of the most effective ways to reduce anger escalation and aggression. If you are still having problems with aggressive behavior – you have *not* effectively implemented the time-out skill. You may think that the time-out is for others and not for you. But, you need to incorporate it and decide to do it. No one can do it for you. You must decide and do it. Go back to the lesson on Taking a Break and plan to take this step the next time you begin to feel tense, irritated, disappointed and frustrated or angry.
The time-out will work because it gives you time to think about the issues, pray, cool down physically and make a plan.

2. *Talking to Yourself*:
In this workbook we talk about how biases, irrational beliefs, impulsivity, cognitive triggers affect anger escalation. What do you tell yourself when some event occurs which irritates you? Do you have "hot self-talk?" Do you say, "He thinks he can bully me" or "they deserve to be punished" or "no one deserves this kind of treatment?" These phrases will escalate your anger. What you tell yourself will affect your choices, actions and any consequences.

What about telling yourself something different such as: "he is having a bad day" or "maybe they didn't know how this would affect me" or "I'm not going to think about this now – I'll take a walk or a break and pray. I'll concentrate on what the real issue is."

Write out what you have said to yourself in the past when you've been irritated or angry:

Write out what you could say to yourself instead:

Write out how you can respond in a healthy way:

3. *Interventions*:
Using the *"Stop and Think"* card. Get a 3x5 card – title it: Stop and Think. Write out some principles, thinking ahead or self-talk phrases which have helped you manage your response to anger and aggressive behavior. Keep this card or post it in several places: your purse, jacket, car, home, office, etc. Write a reminder in your Smart phone, Iphone, Ipad, nook, kindle and computer.

How will this card help you? When you feel frustrated, angry or irritated--read it. Some people incorporate prayer. Use this during a time-out as well. Think about how to respond in a healthy way. If you don't need to respond immediately – then, plan to think more about it later. Return to the person when you are ready with a request or to problem-solve.

More keys to reducing anger:
It is very important to take care of yourself through: Relaxation, Rest, and Nutrition. What makes relaxation, rest and nutrition vital to preventing anger arousal? In the book we talk about how "aversive bodily states" precipitate anger. Low blood sugar, stress, fatigue, sleep deprivation and more trigger anger.

When you have times to relax and enjoy life – go for a hike, a walk or read a book – your body and mind will rejuvenate. You need times of relaxation and appropriate sleep as well. If you are not sleeping well – you will begin the day feeling on-edge. Anything which goes wrong will seem like the "worst thing that could happen." These keys will help decrease anger and thus, prevent aggression.

Foundational Insights:
Changing your self-talk, seeking your Higher Power for guidance and taking a time-out are keys to stopping aggression, reducing and managing anger. Compassion is another key to managing anger. If you care about someone else's needs you will be focusing on how help them versus ruminating about how angry they made you and how much you hurt. It is still true that you need to work through anger and conflict but, you can do it effectively without crushing people or lashing out.

Questions for Thought

1. According to these Insights, what characteristics are we challenged to demonstrate in our relationships?
_____
_____
_____

2. Which intervention: time-out, talking to yourself, faith is most helpful in defusing your anger?
_____
_____
_____

3. Identify areas in your life which hinder you from relaxing, sleeping and healthy eating:
_____
_____
_____
_____

4. What can you do to change this week to incorporate more rest, relaxation, sleep and good nutrition? How might this affect your anger quotient?
_____
_____
_____

5. Which of the keys to stopping aggression or lashing out can you begin to incorporate more in your life?
_____
_____
_____

What if scenarios:
a. *Your friend acts rudely towards you in front of others.*

Your anger quotient is: 1-10 (1=low; 5= moderate; 10=high) _____

Your response is:
_____
_____

What's good about your response (thoughts, behavior)?
_____
_____

Describe the consequences of your response:
_____
_____

How does this help you achieve your goals?
_____
_____

What do you need to change? How could applying one of the skills help the situation?
_____
_____

b. *Your sibling forgets to pay back a loan on time.*
Your anger quotient is: 1-10 (1=low; 5= moderate; 10=high) _____
Your response is:
_____
_____

What's good about your response (thoughts, behavior)?
_____
_____

Describe the consequences of your response:
_____
_____

How does this help you achieve your goals?
_____
_____

What do you need to change? How could applying one of the skills help the situation?
_____
_____

c. *You are standing in line waiting to be checked at the drugstore and someone cuts in.*
Your anger quotient is: 1-10 (1=low; 5= moderate; 10=high) _____
Your response is:
_____
_____

What's good about your response (thoughts, behavior)?
_____
_____

Describe the consequences of your response:
_____
_____

How does this help you achieve your goals?
_____
_____

What do you need to change? How could applying one of the skills help the situation?
_____
_____

ANGER MANAGEMENT PROGRESS REPORT:

Week ___: (copy and use weekly)
1. Anger Survey results (circle one): Category I   Category II   Category III
2. Identify triggers:

3. Identify present coping skill use:

Please measure your use of anger coping skills from 1-10: _____
(1=poor use of skills   5=intermittent use of skills   10=consistent use of skills)

4. How is your anger presently affecting:

School:	greatly	moderately	little	none
Relationships:	greatly	moderately	little	none
Family:	greatly	moderately	little	none
Friends:	greatly	moderately	little	none
Job (if you work):	greatly	moderately	little	none
Legal:	greatly	moderately	little	none
Personal:	greatly	moderately	little	none
Goals:	greatly	moderately	little	none
Other:	greatly	moderately	little	none

(describe other:_____)

5. Describe one angry or frustrated episode/situation from this past week. What happened and with whom?

   What triggered your anger?

   What were your thoughts?

   How did you respond?

   What skill did you try to use? Was it effective?

   Underline the following coping skills from this book & workbook which you could implement in the future? (time-out, assertiveness, problem-solving, let it go, change thinking, forgive, pray, conflict management skills, avoid triggers, etc.) How have you improved?

*Course participants are granted permission to duplicate this page for personal use only.

Case Study: The following exam was completed by a student. Read and answer the questions at the end of this case study.

1. Please identify some of the causes of anger from the book/course:

People for whom getting or being angry is a problem have turned a perfectly good emotion into a lifestyle of continually being and getting angry. In many ways, Anger is a "cover-emotion" since it is rarely a case of simple righteous indignation, but rather a reaction to rejection, attack or a perceived threat. Negative self-talk, poor self-esteem, a desire to control one's surroundings, frustration at not getting one's way are all possible triggers to an angry outburst. Couple these external stimuli with faulty thinking about the external world (i.e. unrealistic expectations about control, or people doing what you want, people ought to let me have my way, etc.) and one is quite quickly angry. After a period of learning these new chemical pathways, the brain will become very efficient at "getting its fix."

2. How does the book/course describe the harmfulness of an angry response?

Anger is most harmful to the person getting angry. Even before an outburst is visible to those in the fall-out zone, the BP and HR have been steadily climbing; the whole fight-flight mechanism has stoked the body's fires preparing for confrontation. That's stressful from a physiological point of view. It makes your parts wear out faster and predisposes you to a wide variety of stress related disorders (i.e. heart attacks or ulcers). In addition, the emotional consequences from hurting those around you can be very hard (and expensive) to endure. Anger is harmful if too frequent, too intense, too long, leads to aggression, or when it disturbs relationships with others (home, work, school, social).

3. How has anger personally harmed your relationships or personal life?

My relationships have been ruined primarily by the angry tone I set. I harbored resentment against my friends and it showed very clearly in the way I dealt with them. I have hurt people's feelings; I have said things I later regretted. I have acted like a small child who does not get his way…only this child has the ability to express himself in ways much more damaging that merely crying and stamping feet. The biggest cost is the alienation that follows. It isolates me from the very people to whom I want to be close. Instead of control, I gained loneliness.

4. In what ways can anger be helpful as described in the book/course?

God wired us to get angry to warn us of danger. Anger lets us know something is wrong and it enables us to flee or to fight if need be for our protection. It alerts us to injustice, helps us recognize boundaries, and energizes us for action. The chemical pathways exist for very good reasons, but they are powerful and our brain chemistry will actually change with frequent outbursts. Even Jesus got angry. He was fully God and fully man. When he chased the money changers out of the temple, he was angry…but he committed no sin. This idea that we can be angry and not sin is much harder tightrope to walk for us humans of lesser mettle. It's really hard to think clearly when all the blood gets pumped to our extremities and adrenaline flows through our body.

5. What are some of the major triggers of anger described in the book/course?

Cognitive triggers and physiological triggers: The first is a thinking problem; the second is one of biology. Our ability to cope with stress is related to how we think and feel. How we think about what we observe affects the conclusions we reach. If we think people are out to get us and some guy in cuts us off on the freeway, we immediately react as though the act is a personal attack…when in point of fact, he is so self-focused, he doesn't even know we are there. Biases, irrational beliefs, impulsivity, and skill deficits all contribute to angry outbursts.

Our reserve capacity for dealing with any external influence is also gated by how our body is functioning. Sleep, food, hormonal balance, and mental tension all contribute to our response.

6. What, specifically, triggers your anger?

Mostly whacked thinking that seems perfectly reasonable at the time. For a variety of reasons, small distortions of the truth get included in our filter through which we observe the world. The distortions affect the way we view the world, much like a smudge of grease on a window would obscure one's view of the outdoors. My anger is almost always an overreaction to incorrect thinking.

7. How did you recently control your anger?

I stopped the cycle. If I missed seeing the trigger setup early enough to just avoid the trap, I know what I feel like when I am starting to get angry. When I start to feel even a little like that, I just call for a time out or I pause and remind myself of how important it is to remain in control of myself, not the other person.

Recently, I was having an emotionally charged discussion with my girlfriend. This of course means that we both felt strongly about the topic and had opposing viewpoints. I was able to look ahead and see how the conversation was going to unfold so I stopped talking. I started asking questions to understand her view point.

This is much easier to do when I remind myself that she is not trying to hurt me, she really cares about me, and she wants the best for both of us. It's amazing what some corrected thinking can accomplish

8. How did you change or challenge the triggers which make you angry?

I do not need to be in control of people around me. I can only control me. I can't control them. Most of the time, they are not even aware of me and are busy worrying about their own set of problems, so chances are it isn't about me (whatever they might be doing that bugs me). Finally I observed that it is arrogant to think people are doing things "to" me. This implies that they spend a lot of time thinking about me. I'm not THAT important. Life is full of disappointments and failed plans…that's normal. In the grand scheme, it's insignificant…not a reason to get angry. Last but not least, as I get healthier, I am realizing I can be frustrated or upset about something without becoming angry. I like to say, "The burner of my soul, once again, has OFF, SIMMER, MED and HI; instead of just OFF and HI."

9. What new coping skills have you recently used from this book/course to manage your anger? Which was most beneficial?

I have started asking myself the question: "Is my anger justified?" Usually the answer is "No." Addressing the core issue: "Why am I feeling this way?" Asking myself, "What is true?" Allowing more time to process before drawing a conclusion. Choosing to express my views and thoughts constructively, instead of being confrontational. I find that implementing the thinking-acting cycle takes longer, but is very beneficial. I remain calm and then it is much easier to see the salient issues from the red herrings.

10. In what ways have you discovered that God can help you manage anger?

He reminds me constantly of how patient he is with me. My job is not to help him with his. My job is to become more like him by extending grace to those around me. By giving grace freely, it frees me of the need to correct or punish. This is some nutty thinking, but God is faithful and he is helping me to dig away the distractions to get to the root of these kinds of distortions.

11. What can you do this next week to manage your anger more effectively?

Extend grace and practice responding to external events…not reacting

12. How has this course helped you personally understand and manage anger?

This course has provided more insight, new and different tools for lessening the rate at which these feelings develop, and in some ways preventing the feelings all together as is the case with faulty thinking about external events.

Case study questions:

1. What are Bob's issues? What are triggers and causes of his anger?

2. What are the consequences Bob experiences from his anger?

3. What insights does Bob gain about himself and controlling anger?

4. What coping skills are most effective for Bob? When does he apply empathy?

5. In what ways does Bob change his thinking and perspective to defuse anger and conflict?

6. Can you identify with Bob? What have you learned from his story?

PRACTICE ACTIVITIES for ASSERTIVE RESPONSES:
Remember that the ASERT scripts are to help guide you through the process of bringing up and working through issues in a respectful way. Not every step is necessary as some situations need only an explanation of the problem and feelings. Many situations can be resolved by requesting a change. Here are some completed examples to guide you through the process:

1. *When your sibling is too lazy and doesn't do his/her fair share of the chores...*
Use ASERT:
Approach calmly and respectfully:

State the Problem: State the facts. Let your sibling know what is bothering you. Be as objective and specific as possible. Use simple concrete terms to describe their behavior. Be specific.

Express feelings: Express to him/her what you think and fell about his/her behavior in a specific situation. Acknowledge that those are your feelings. Aim for clarity about your feelings. Avoid provoking feelings of guilt. Ex: "I feel stressed out when you don't do your part of the household chores every day" or "I am upset because you didn't clean up the kitchen after you ate."

Request change & feedback: "Please take out the trash as you agreed to." "I would appreciate it if you would clean up after yourself so I don't have to do it."

State how this will benefit you and your relationship. "This will really help me feel less stressed out and improve family relationships."

Talk it out (consequences/options): You may want to talk more about household chores and how to fairly divide them.

2. *Someone in your group regularly tries to make perverted or cruel jokes. Sometimes they call you 'racist' or other names.*
Use ASERT:
Approach calmly and respectfully: No blaming or shaming.

State the Problem: "I find these types of jokes offensive and degrading."

Express feelings: "These jokes make me feel uneasy and are offensive to me."

Request change & feedback: "I like to joke around to but, prefer humor that is clean and non-judgmental."

State how this will benefit you and your relationship. I hope that you will respect my request since this is necessary for us to continue and have a healthy friendship.

Talk it out (consequences/options): You may decide that this person's humor is too objectionable, that the relationship is unhealthy and you need to part ways with this person.

3. *When your sister or brother doesn't clean up food after him/herself so you can't use the table.*
Use ASERT:
Approach calmly and respectfully:

State the Problem: "When you don't clean the table after yourself – I can't use it to do my homework." "It makes a mess and I feel responsible to clean it up."

Express feelings: "When I have to clean up after you I feel aggravated and unappreciated."

Request change & feedback: "Please put your dishes away and throw out old food. Maybe you would like to request a change from me?"
"I appreciate the fact that you listened to me and said you will try to make a change."

State how this will benefit you and your relationship. "If you start doing this – I can finish my homework and we can play some games."

Talk it out (consequences/options): You may want to discuss other areas of household chores and how you can work more as a team.

Now, complete the following scenarios using this approach.

4. *Your friend often is texting or surfing the internet while you are trying to talk to them*
Use ASERT:
Approach calmly and respectfully:
State the Problem:
_____
_____

Express feelings:
_____
_____

Request change & feedback:
_____
_____

State how this will benefit you and your relationship.
_____
_____

Talk it out (consequences/options)

5. *A friend criticized you for no reason in front of others.*
Use ASERT:
Approach calmly and respectfully:

State the Problem:
_____
_____

Express feelings:
_____
_____

Request change & feedback:
_____
_____

State how this will benefit you and your relationship.
_____
_____

Talk it out (consequences/options)

6. *Your parent has been very irritable with you—demanding you do more than your fair-share of chores around the house. It's interfering with your heavy-load of homework.* You use ASERT:
Approach calmly and respectfully:

State the Problem:
_____
_____

Express feelings:
_____
_____

Request change & feedback:
_____
_____

State how this will benefit you and your relationship.
_____
_____

Talk it out (consequences/options)

7. *Your lab partner has been fooling around in class and not doing his/her part of the project. You bring up the issue by using* ASERT:

Approach calmly and respectfully:

State the Problem:
_____
_____

Express feelings:
_____
_____

Request change & feedback:
_____
_____

State how this will benefit you and your relationship.
_____
_____

Talk it out (consequences/options)

8. *A teacher talked harshly to you and penalized you for some infraction which you were not a part of.* Use ASERT:

Approach calmly and respectfully:

State the Problem:
_____
_____

Express feelings:
_____
_____

Request change & feedback:
_____
_____

State how this will benefit you and your relationship.
_____
_____

Talk it out (consequences/options)

9. *Write a current issue or concern you need to bring up to someone such as a friend or family member using* ASERT:

Approach calmly and respectfully:

State the Problem:
_____
_____

Express feelings:
_____
_____

Request change & feedback:
_____
_____

State how this will benefit you and your relationship.
_____
_____

Talk it out (consequences/options)

Questions for Thought

a. What have you learned by using the ASERT model?
_____
_____
_____
_____

b. When have you applied this approach to a real life situation? Describe the consequences and any changes that could have been made.
_____
_____
_____
_____
_____

What's Good About Anger? Expanded Book & Workbook for Teens

Cognitive strategies Activity Sheet: These strategies or reminders are used to guide behavior during the provocation itself or to counter irrational beliefs that set the stage for overreaction.

Thinking ahead reminders: The purpose of self-talk reminders is to help you make more deliberate and adaptive choices when confronted with a provocation (Feindler and Ecton). From a neural perspective – you are prompting higher brain center activities located in the verbal left-hemisphere region to control or override emotional reactions of the lower limbic regions.

Reminders interfere with impulsivity in 2 major ways: coping self-talk is an incompatible behavior that blocks the processing of "hot" thoughts. Second, reminders can be prompts to activate predetermined coping efforts. Sample reminders:

Approaching the situation:
Generate alternative response options and weigh the long-term consequences of each. This process has been shown to produce better responses. Rehearse reminders "out loud" during role-play situations.
- Keep your breathing even.
- What is it that I have to do?
- Take one step at a time.
- Stick to the issue and don't take it personally.

During the confrontation:
- Just exhale slowly.
- Remember not to take it personally.
- He/she might want me to get angry but I'm going to one-up him/her by staying cool.
- What is the issue really? Keep it in perspective.
- Just state your needs clearly. Stick to "I" statement. No blaming-that won't help.
- Acknowledge his/her point. That can help sometimes.
- Getting real mad will cost me. I'll be a chump. Stay calm-be a champ.
- No one is right or wrong. We just have different needs.
- If there's nothing I can do now, just chill-out. It will be over soon. Ride the wave.

The following leads may be useful: What would you tell a friend to calm down in a situation?
- What could you tell yourself to "chill-out" your body?
- What would you ideally want to do? What could you say to yourself to accomplish this?

Thinking ahead reminders:
Self-talk can also curb impulsivity by helping the individual anticipate consequences. Thinking ahead reminders or problem solving may be particularly applicable as an individual considers a course of action when there is an impulse to become aggressive. Examples of typical thinking ahead reminders:
- What's going to happen if….
- Is it really worth it?
- Is making myself look tough now worth it for what it'll cost me?
- Will this make a difference in a week?
- What might be some things I could do or say?

Belief Inventory (resource: BARK manual, Dr. Gary Gintner)

For each statement circle the number that best indicates how characteristic the item is for you:

	Disagree a lot			Agree a lot	
1. I must have approval from people I care about.	1	2	3	4	5
2. I must perform at a high level or I'm disappointed in myself.	1	2	3	4	5
3. My emotional upset is from external pressures that I have little ability to control.	1	2	3	4	5
4. It is easier to avoid challenges than to face them.	1	2	3	4	5
5. I can't stand it if someone says something negative to me.	1	2	3	4	5
6. I frequently don't get what I deserve even though I worked for it.	1	2	3	4	5
7. I'm often treated unfairly.	1	2	3	4	5
8. Others are frequently provoking me for no good reason.	1	2	3	4	5
9. If you don't hit someone back after they insult you, you will be the target of more insults in the future.	1	2	3	4	5
10. I like to be in control in a relationship.	1	2	3	4	5
11. I get irritated when others don't do something the way I expect it to be done.	1	2	3	4	5
12. I get very angry when I don't get what I want.	1	2	3	4	5
13. When people love you, you shouldn't have to ask for things.	1	2	3	4	5

Notes

This comprehensive book & workbook provides several references or paraphrases from the Holy Bible for greater insights and examples into anger and healthy responses to it.

Lesson Two:
1. Ephesians 4:25

Lesson Three:
1. James 1:19
2. Proverbs 22:24
3. Proverbs 15:1

Lesson Five:
1. Nehemiah 5:6-7
2. James 1:19

Lesson Seven:
1. Colossians 3:12-14
2. I Corinthians 13:4-5

Lesson Eight:
1. Colossians 3:13

Lesson Nine:
1. James 1:19

Lesson Ten:
1. Philippians 4:8

BIBLIOGRAPHY

Ali, Dr. Amir. The Article Collection of M. Amir Ali, Ph.D. "Forgiveness." Date of access: February 2, 2006. <http://www.ilaam.net/Forgiveness.html> a personal website.

Backus, William. Hidden Rift With God. Minneapolis, MN: Bethany House, 1990.

Burns, D. Feeling Good. New York: Signet, 1980.

Carlson, Dwight L., M.D. Overcoming Hurts & Anger. Eugene, OR: Harvest House, 1981.

Dobson, Dr. James and Dobson, Shirley. Night Light : A Devotional for Couples. Sisters, OR: Multnomah, Inc., 2000.

Feindler, E.L. and Ecton, R.B. Adolescent Anger Control: Cognitive-Behavioral Techniques. New York: Pergamon Press, 1986.

Gintner, Dr. Gary. Behavioral Anger Reduction Kit (BARK). Louisiana State University, 1995. Used by permission. E-mail: gintner@lsu.edu. Our thanks to Dr. Gintner for the use of his manual's statistics, anger triggers, the process of anger and thinking ahead reminders.

Goleman, Daniel. Working with Emotional Intelligence. New York: Bantam Books, 2000.

Hauck, Dr. Paul A. Overcoming Frustration and Anger. Westminster John Knox Press; Dimensions, 1974.

Holmes, T.H. and Rahe, R.H. "The Social Readjustment Rating Scale." Journal of Psychosomatic Research, 11:213-218, 1967.

Hoy, L. and Griffin, T. What's Good About Anger? Fourth Edition, Oak Brook, IL. CounselCare Connection, P.C., 2016

Kendall, R.T. Total Forgiveness. Lake Mary, FL: Charisma House, 2007.

McKay, M., Rogers, P.D. and McKay, J. When Anger Hurts: Quieting the Storm Within. Oakland: New Harbinger, 1989.

Potter-Efron, Ron. Handbook of Anger Management. New York: Haworth Press, 2005.

Potegal, M., Stemmler, G., Spielberger, C. International Handbook of Anger. New York: Springer, 2010.

Prager, Dennis. "Response." The Sunflower. New York: Schocken Books, 1998. 225-30.

Yancey, Philip. "An Unnatural Act." Christianity Today. 8 April 1991: 36-39.

ABOUT THE AUTHORS

Lynette J. Hoy is a Licensed Clinical Professional Counselor in the state of Illinois, a National Certified Counselor and a credentialed Anger Management Specialist-V, Diplomate, Supervisor and Consultant with the National Anger Management Association. Mrs. Hoy is also a Board Certified Professional Christian Counselor, a crisis counselor and domestic violence advocate. Lynette has counseled and trained hundreds of clients, couples, and students in anger management. She has trained and certified hundreds of counselors, professionals, and leaders in anger management. Lynette presents various classes, workshops, and marriage seminars. She and her husband David have been married over forty-six years and have one married daughter. Lynette's experience of growing up in an abusive home and then counseling clients struggling with anger has provided the motivation for writing the What's Good About Anger? books, various anger management articles, workbooks, and training manuals. Lynette's faith in God gave her a foundation for loving and forgiving her father.

Ted Griffin worked as Senior Editor of Crossway Books, a division of Good News Publishers, for thirty years and is currently retired. He has authored numerous gospel tracts, including the best-selling You're Special, and is working on several books. He is a mentor, small group facilitator, and adult Sunday school teacher at Calvary Memorial Church in Oak Park, Illinois. He and his wife, Lois, (deceased) were been married for over 45 years and have two grown children and five grandchildren. Having grown up under an alcoholic father, he has personally struggled with and has extensively studied anger issues.

Anyone desiring to contact the authors is invited to do so: Anger Management Institute, 1200 Harger Rd. Suite 602, Oak Brook, IL 60523. Or email Lynette Hoy at: counselor@hoyweb.com & Ted Griffin at: twordsmith@aol.com

Anger Management Institute Resources and Programs
1. What's Good About Anger? First edition: for readers and leaders seeking a Christian perspective on and approach to anger. (2014)
2. What's Good About Anger? Putting Your Anger to Work for Good Fourth Edition (for a general readership) with FAQs. Foreword by Dr. Richard Pfeiffer. (2016)
3. What's Good About Anger? Expanded Book/Workbook 16 Lessons (2016) for adults and Expanded Book/Workbook for teens. Healing the Wounds of Anger in Marriage (2015).
4. Anger management certificate courses for individuals needing personal growth or who are required to fulfill court, school or employer orders for anger management.
5. Anger Management Trainer-Specialist Certificate Programs. live workshops; home-study courses for counselors, law enforcement or probation officers, educators, professionals, lay leaders and group facilitators. Approved and endorsed by the National Anger Management Association for obtaining certification as an Anger Management Specialist. Workshops approved by NBCC, NASW for 12 CE/CEUs and IAODAPCA for 13 CEUs. Home-study and online programs approved by NBCC and IAODAPCA for 12 CEUs.
6. What's Good About Anger? DVD seminar with Lynette Hoy, NCC, LCPC, CAMS-V and Steve Yeschek, LCSW, CAMS-IV.

Visit the Anger Management Institute site for all resources and the shopping mall at www.whatsgoodaboutanger.com for ordering information. For any questions contact Lynette Hoy at 630.368.1880, ext. 1 or lynettehoy@gmail.com

Made in the USA
Columbia, SC
18 July 2017